ASPERKIDS

An Insider's Guide to Loving, Understanding and Teaching Children with Asperger Syndrome

Jennifer Cook O'Toole

Foreword by Liane Holliday Willey

Jessica Kingsley *Publishers*
London and Philadelphia

First published in 2012
by Jessica Kingsley Publishers
116 Pentonville Road
London N1 9JB, UK
and
400 Market Street, Suite 400
Philadelphia, PA 19106, USA

www.jkp.com

Copyright © Jennifer Cook O'Toole 2012
Foreword copyright © Liane Holliday Willey 2012
Cover art by Brian Bojanowski

Library of Congress Cataloging in Publication Data
A CIP catalog record for this book is available from the Library of Congress

British Library Cataloguing in Publication Data
A CIP catalogue record for this book is available from the British Library

ISBN 978 1 84905 902 2
eISBN 978 0 85700 647 9

Printed and bound in the United States

"Fresh, honest, organic and raw insights – Jennifer has written a legacy for all those on the spectrum, inviting everyone into an intricate and delicious mindset of an Asperfamily's challenges and successes. This book is a literary feast of new and exciting creative ideas and strategies which are shared in a very unique conversational manner. This book may be the key to unlocking a new and successful way of teaching and communicating with persons on the spectrum."

– Josie Santomauro, mother of a son with Asperger syndrome, editor of Autism All-Stars: How We Use Our Autism and Asperger Traits to Shine in Life and co-author of Set for Success: Activities for Teaching Emotional, Social and Organisational Skills

"Asperkids is brilliant! Not only is Jennifer an inspiring person, she's an Aspermom out to make a difference. Her passion to educate the NT world about Aspies shines through. Many Asperkids, and their families, will benefit from her personal insight. I am convinced this book will make a positive impact."

– Julie Clark, author of Asperger's in Pink: Pearls of Wisdom from Inside the Bubble of Raising a Child with Asperger's

"Jennifer provides a unique perspective into the world of Asperger syndrome – helping to put all the pieces together, with a little humor thrown in along the way. I will highly recommend this book to any Asperparent to better understand their child's world and help them grow, learn, and develop based on their unique strengths."

– Courtney Enos, MS-OT, occupational therapist, Touchstone Therapy, North Carolina, USA

"Amazing! Jennifer's ability to share her Asperger perspective and explain what our kids need most in the home and in school is fantastic. She gets right to what matters and makes powerful points that have to be heard. On both a personal and a professional level, I say this is a book that needs to be on shelves everywhere."

– Meredith G. Bove, MBA, Educational Strategies Consultant and mother of a son with Asperger syndrome

"Jennifer Cook O'Toole's personal understanding of the Asperger 'profile' makes Asperkids a fascinating read. In it she gives a wealth of exciting and innovative 'detours' around the challenges of AS and has provided a book full of lively and enthusiastic ideas to get you really enjoying working with your Asperger child. This is one of the most respectful books about teaching children with Asperger syndrome I have read and I thoroughly recommend it."

– *Clare Lawrence, teacher, autism worker, mother, and author of* Autism and Flexischooling: A Shared Classroom and Homeschooling Approach *and* How to Make School Make Sense: A Parents' Guide to Helping the Child with Asperger Syndrome

"*Asperkids* has touched my heart to its deepest core, brought tears to my eyes, knowledge to my mind and an in-depth understanding of Asperger syndrome. It is beautifully written, easy to understand and incredibly sincere. I will most definitely stock the shelves of our psychological book store with this wonderful, insightful book. Kudos to Jennifer Cook O'Toole for her passion, love, and knowledge of Asperger syndrome and her willingness and eagerness to share it with everyone."

– *Diane Chartrand-Balcer, Purchasing Director for Insomnia Bookstore (Asperger syndrome and psychology specialists), North Carolina, USA*

"*Asperkids* is a gift to parents of kids with Asperger syndrome and to all the professionals who teach and work with these complicated and wonderful children. O'Toole reminds us that with the right tools and understanding, the challenge of teaching children with AS can be easy and exciting. Her unique perspective as an individual with AS, as a parent of multiple children with AS, and as an experienced teacher, makes this a must-read for anyone who wants to understand more about Asperger syndrome."

– *Ann Palmer, author of* A Friend's and Relative's Guide to Supporting the Family with Autism *and* Realizing the College Dream with Autism or Asperger Syndrome, *and faculty member, The Carolina Institute for Developmental Disabilities, University of North Carolina, USA*

"As a neurotypical mom with two kids with Asperger syndrome, *Asperkids* gave me an inside look into the minds of my own children. Jennifer's unique viewpoint really helped me understand how I can communicate better with my kids, support their talents, and help them navigate the world. *Asperkids* should serve as a touchstone for parents and teachers alike. I'll definitely be sharing this book!"

– *Joslyn Gray, autism advocate and author of the blog* stark. raving. mad. mommy.

For My Father, Joe

Look, Daddy, I'm dancing.

"I dwell in Possibility"
—*Emily Dickinson*

CONTENTS

FOREWORD

Just a few pages into *Asperkids*, I knew I was reading something special. Jennifer Cook O'Toole's writing eased me into feeling as though I were having a charming conversation with a trusted old friend. It is so easy to settle into O'Toole's words, which are rich and well crafted, attentive and honoring, even when they are speaking of the sad bits we Aspies will inevitably struggle with. It is also easy to quickly recognize O'Toole knows what she is talking about. She is clearly a gifted thinker and uplifting member of the Asperger community who has worked hard to figure out the world she struggled with as a child. She is a remarkable tutor who can teach Aspertalk to neurotypicals so they will fully understand the importance of seeing the world through Aspie eyes. And she is a devoted mother and social worker who helps parents and society predict when their Asperkid may fall so they will know how to save them from hurt and help them to love the gifts that make them Aspie.

Asperkids is a book about advocacy as much as it is a book about understanding and assisting children with Asperger syndrome. For example, the book discusses how difficult it can be for Asperkids and their families to stand up to bullies in the playground, as well as authority figures who would have us believe our gut instincts and parental decisions are off-base and clouded. We read first-hand accounts of the misunderstandings society has concerning our kids in general, and the typical ramifications of those misunderstandings. A much-needed ray of light is shed on the differences between Aspergirls and Asperboys. O'Toole also elucidates on the complexities of Aspie friendships and then provides insight into how to find and maintain relationships that can become mutually enriching. Each chapter, in fact, holds a follow-up section filled with insightful learning and social designs that will support our kids. All in all, a comprehensive read on Asperkids.

Before you know it, you will be finished with this book and though you will have oodles of fresh perspectives on Asperger syndrome and piles of new ideas and strategies to offer anyone interested in helping our kids, you will wish you had more pages to turn, because with each page comes a new anecdote that turns into a creative learning experience that morphs into a helpful curriculum guide and faithful manual for Asperkids! O'Toole is the real deal bundle of experience and knowledge our Asperger community can turn to for compassionate understanding and wise advice. I can't wait for her next book.

Liane Holliday Willey, EdD
Author of Pretending to be Normal: Living with Asperger's Syndrome *and* Asperger Safety Skills for Women: How to Save a Perfectly Good Female Life

ACKNOWLEDGMENTS

I never would have thought of writing this book without the insistent encouragement of some pretty amazing professionals. So, with great admiration and fondness, I must thank Drs. Irm Bellavia, Stephanie Kemper, Lynn Vivian, Tracy Barcott, and Anthony Patterson. For the direction you have given my life and the value you made me see in myself, thank you.

Behind every good woman…is a bunch of equally awesome women friends. Thank you: to "playgroup," Amanda, Prof. Elizabeth, Lauren, Eva, and Melanie, my first readers – I love you always. To Aileen, for your creative genius and endless taco salad. To Lori, for being my "sister," even a ridiculous amount of years later. You are all proof that family isn't limited by blood. And to all the friends and family whose encouragement has absolutely blown me away…my heart is overflowing.

To the amazing Jessica Kingsley of Jessica Kingsley Publishers: it seems an unbelievable blessing that my manuscript managed to land in front of you. Every bit of this book – and me as a writer – is better for your ideas and direction. Thank you, Emily McClave and Katelynn Bartleson, for getting the word out about such important kids. And you, Vicki Peters and Christine Firth, for the enormous impact of your intricate efforts, and for your warmth to this American "rookie." THANK YOU ALL. You are helping me to leave the world better than when I got here. Thank you for taking a chance on a new voice, and for putting such strong support behind me.

Mom, I admire your courage in allowing me to share such an intimate story. Thank you for seeing the potential in me, the work-in-progress. Daddy, I miss you beyond words, yet hear you so often. This book is truly your legacy for me and for your grandchildren. So for everything, I love you, Mom and Daddy.

I would never have felt the import of writing a single word were it not for my children. Now, Mama's words are forever here for you to remember how powerfully I love you, and how precious you are in God's eyes. You make me laugh at every day, and joyfully share the dance parties by my side. Thank you, Maura, Sean, and Gavin, for being mine. Mommy loves you…more.

Last, to my funny, hunky, steady husband: John, I still look at you and feel the flutter of new love. I am so grateful for your bravery in the adventure and in your candor on behalf of our children. Thank you for being my best friend every day – good and bad – and for showing me that this was the moment to change everything. With your arms around me, it is and always will be "a wonderful world."

INTRODUCTION
How Asperger's Saved My Life

The single most important lesson my mother ever taught me was spoken from the doorway of my bedroom just after I had had a major meltdown. It was two weeks before my senior year of college was to begin, and I had to get back – there was an honors thesis to write, sorority work to accomplish, packing to do.

But I was not exactly ready to pick out a duvet cover. Only two weeks before, I had ended a dating relationship that was abusive in every way you could imagine. I drove the three hours to my parents' house, and completely fell apart. My brain is one that demands logic, and for the life of me, I could not figure out what I had done so wrong that had made my world implode. So, I did what I always do when life throws me a curveball. I research. A lot. Facts are comforting. They make sense out of chaos.

Late one sleepless night, I caught a television announcement about dating violence, inviting viewers in trouble to call their information hotline; and I did call – right away – asking for any literature they could send. When the thick manila envelopes arrived, I buried myself in the information inside. There were charts and blueprints, clearly reoccurring patterns of interpersonal behavior – that most confusing of subjects. Suddenly, things which had been nebulous and fuzzy were organized and logical. Light bulbs flashed above my head, and the relief flooded over me – in collecting and analyzing data, I had been able to make sense of the endless cycle that had bound my life for almost two years. Feelings were fuzzy, motivations unclear. I never would have been able to make sense of the interpersonal craziness that had broken me. And now, after months of confusion and tumult, a few simple diagrams and reams of information had fixed everything for me. I didn't realize it then, but that was my if/then, logic-seeking, fact-collecting Aspie mind taking over. Delivering me from the depths of depression and self-doubt, Asperger's had just saved my life.

Now, here I sat in the center of my bed, surrounded by pamphlets and papers, crying with some absolute mess of totally conflicting emotions. "The best way to get out of your own head and make sense of your experiences," my mom said from the doorway, "is to do something with them for someone else." She was absolutely right. It was that simple. If I had information or perspective that could make someone else's life better, it was my responsibility to share it.

One week later, I was back on campus, quickly establishing myself as the first college representative on the state's Coalition Against Domestic Violence. I set up a talking series, support groups, liaisons with government agencies and university administration. I was interviewed by several newspapers, I trained medical students, and heard stories few others did. From there, I was hired to be a full-time domestic violence counselor for the police department in the southern city of Charlotte, North Carolina. I gave speeches at universities, in hospitals, and at roll-calls, hosted "Makeover Days for Survivors" and conferences, and managed to marry an (amazingly handsome and wonderful) police officer along the way.

My little shoebox of special tokens still contains notes and cards from extraordinary women along that journey. They spoke of my bravery, of all that they learned from me – but I would honestly tell you that I am not so special. It all began that day, surrounded by brochures and information. I just did what my mom told me to do, in the way my Aspie brain made me do it.

Throughout my life, that Aspie pattern of live, research, and share has continued to be my method of making sense of many things. And making sense of a situation, like closing a door or righting an error, is *very* important to us Aspies.

My eight-year-old daughter is a Make-A-Wish kid who has been battling a cascade of multisystem failures since infancy. I have seen horrific things happen to small people, and listened to doctors who truly had no idea what the future held. So I did my thing. I researched, and researched. On many occasions, doctors have asked me where I went to med school – with absolutely no condescension. I don't have my MD, but I do have my MOM with at least as many hours of investigating and fact-finding under my belt. And then, I shared. For two years, I was lucky enough to serve on the family advisory board at our local children's hospital. In that capacity, it was our charge to educate every single medical professional – from nursing assistants to attending doctors – on the perspective of the patients' families. Gratefully, I can even say that my rendition of my daughter's journey was the one chosen to be the "poster" story for a year. I advised online medical groups, blogged for thousands of readers, and generally, as I did years earlier, tried to take the struggle in my life and use it to make the world a better place for anyone listening. I've been told that it worked. So, in a sense, Aspie thinking saved my daughter's life, too, and our sanity. It may have even eased the burdens of families I will never meet. And to me, that makes everything make sense.

This book is only the latest round, I see now, of that cyclic path I take. It is my next chance to leave a legacy of hope, understanding, and effective change.

Asperger syndrome is tough. If you are reading this book, you probably already know that. The psychological and behavioral pattern it describes has been around forever. But by finally naming that profile, we who fit it are able to make sense of the differences we always knew were there. We can collect data about Asperger's – read books, websites, interviews – and in doing so, recognize ourselves. We can make sense of the ostracism, gaffes, and self-doubt with better understanding and maybe even a little bit of mercy. I, like so many people – my husband, my three children, and, I believe, my late father – am an Aspie.

For better, worse, and in between, I have lived it, and researched it. Knowing more, I have done better for myself and for my children. Now, they are being educated in a way that makes sense to their little minds. They are supported in ways that give them the tools they need to succeed while never seeking to change the wonderful people they already are. This is the story of why I understand the ways in which

Asperkids learn, think, and feel more accurately than a neurotypical person might; it is also the memoir of how I developed effective strategies for learning and living based on real life. Everything I do for my children and students is informed by Asperger's. It has to be; it is who we are. Within the coming pages, I hope my own personal narratives will inspire parents, and that accessible pedagogical tools will empower teachers, therapists, and caregivers. Like advice from a friend who's been there (and still *is* there), I want this book to change society's view of these precious (and precocious) children.

Every strategy that follows for learning and living with Asperger's is credible and powerful because it is borne of my own life's journey, or that of my children. As you read on, I hope you find peace in the Aspie perspectives and insights I give, inspiration in the educational methods and life strategies I've created, and a real sense that everything is going to be different, but it's going to be OK. I'm absolutely going to give it to you "real." No fluffy pretense or bandwagon ribbon parties. The truth is tough, but it's the truth. And you deserve to know: it's gonna be good.

May my Asperfamily's gift to you be the love you finally recognize, the passions you are able to appreciate, and the future you can build. This journey we will take together is more than another chance for me to share a blessing hidden within a trial. This is a story of understanding, love, and compassion from one generation to another, from one parent to another, from one teacher to another, from one Aspie to another. I think like you do. I think like they do, too. So let's get to speaking Asperger's – the natives may be quirky and challenging, but I promise, we're a whole lot of fun once you get to know us a little better. Welcome.

1 THE THEORY OF MY MIND
How Asperkids Think

The unexpected redhead

"She's got red hair!"

This was, apparently, the first thing my mother ever said upon seeing me. She was merely surprised, she has always explained. She hadn't expected a little redhead (even though she says she had been "Titian-haired" as a girl). But then again, what we expect and what really is are often not quite the same, are they?

The ginger hair did continue to be my calling card, though. I learned throughout my childhood that this unique feature was the source of quite a lot of attention. It was a pretty, coppery color which adults constantly admired, and as I got older, turned quite a few glances my way. Per cliché, perhaps, I was perpetually cast as the femme fatale in school plays, wrote my high school thesis on the history of redheads, and – apparently – was the turnaround answer to my husband's prayers. Just days before we met, he asked God to please send him a special someone, and "if she could be a redhead, that'd be even better."

Being different can make you special. A stand-out. Desired. It can be part of your identity in wonderful ways.

But I know of many other redheads who had quite different experiences. They were the butt of jokes and called names, or they simply hated the attention their ginger locks brought them.

For them, the "different" that nature endowed upon them (quite without their request, mind you) was altogether unwelcome and maybe even resented.

Different can do that, too. It can cast you in a role and include you, if you'll play along. It can discard you instantly when you don't.

And such is the label "Aspie." Without my knowing it, my need for a script to follow, my hyperfocus on details and Mensa-level IQ, my profound loneliness and social naivety were all the product of being different. Yes – they were part of being "Aspie," a word not exactly commonplace in the 1980s or 1990s.

So time goes on. Years pass. Another mother, another daughter.

"She has Asperger syndrome."

This time, it was my voice speaking, now as the mother, seeing an unexpected but familiar reality in the child who is my own little girl. This "different" was unrequested, too, a simple genetic expression as much as my red hair had been. And yet, honestly, in my daughter I had long since recognized the most personal, vulnerable parts of me that had set me apart, for better and for worse. It is an identity that has made us both stand out, both brilliantly and flinchingly.

A little fiery, a lot intense, passionate, and driven. Those descriptors have followed me my whole life long. They resonated as I graduated with honors from a top-tier, Ivy League university, studied graduate level social work and education, and became Mommy to a Make-A-Wish kid. They have done great good for the world, made me a loyal wife and champion for my children. They have also left me completely alone along the way, lost as to what I have done wrong, or how I have messed up. If only people were as simple as formulas, sentence structure, or historical fiction, I would have had it all figured out long ago.

I can't tell you what it's like to be a redhead any more than I can tell you what it is to be Aspie. It is who I am, and I know it innately, intrinsically, inherently. I know nothing else of reality but through careful observation and study. But it is that same tendency to analyze details others ignore, and to remain (hyper)vigilant on behalf of those I love that has forced me to fill a void in the educational and life skills needs of Aspie kids – first, specifically, my own.

In 2010, at an autism conference, I heard Tony Attwood say, "Don't let the brilliance blind you to the challenges." My kids *are* brilliant, endearing, and lovely. They are also abrasive, learning challenged, and obstinate. I have looked and read and listened and questioned, but nowhere could I find answers to their disparate academic, social, and practical living abilities. How could a child read with the fluency of someone ten years her senior, yet not be able to negotiate the morning routine of getting successfully from the car to locker to classroom without tears? She could build Lego® versions of the Empire State Building, but couldn't write legibly enough for anyone to read. How could a little boy of four years do multiplication but not be able to figure out how to get through the steps of successfully using the bathroom when the time came? My kids were like Swiss cheese – powerful, but full of holes.

Though she read multi-chapter books by age three and sounded (to quote her preschool teacher) "like a little professor," my daughter was bounced between five classrooms in two years between the ages of five and seven – and this in the most expensive schools in the city. Too "smart" for one grade level but too socially immature or unfocused for another, she was tossed around with little regard for the psychological impact upon her. No "expert" knew how to manage a child with skill sets spread so far across the charts. Nights filled with tears and mornings with tantrums.

Her little brother was following suit exactly. He was already an encyclopedic expert in superheroes, then planes, then dinosaurs, but couldn't play alongside buddies without turning into the playground rule enforcer, and had meltdowns if he had to sit on a different letter on the classroom's alphabet rug. By the time the little guy was three, we pulled him from preschool to try other special education options, but nothing jelled for them. No one curriculum, school, theory, or approach seemed successful, and between running from therapist to therapist and school to supplemental activities to try to make it all better, the family was emotionally, physically, and financially exhausted.

Eventually, a confluence of unrelated medical and psycho-educational demands had us pull the plug. We would have to homeschool. My background in teaching kids with learning differences as well as in social work kicked in, as did my own life experiences. It was mine to make up. Improvise. Invent. Show time. Game on.

We, like most families with special needs kids, have a lot of professionals involved intimately in our lives – sometimes uncomfortably so. Between endless appointments, assessments, interventions, reassessments, advice, and opinions on every aspect of life from toileting to the state of the marriage, there isn't a lot of room for privacy, or for just *being* versus always *doing* – a simple thing that neurotypical families probably never much consider.

Still, we respect learned opinions and professional dedication. Over the years, our family has accumulated an amazing team of experts whose willingness to think outside of the box is both exciting and challenging. Needless to say, this unexpected educational byway had me extremely self-conscious. I had confidence that I knew my kids best, that I was dedicated to them as no one else could be – but I was still uneasy, I promise you. What would all "the professionals" think of what I could or couldn't do? Really, though, what was there to do but try? So, typically me, I took that challenge and ran.

Improvising

Isn't it the way of the world that when we finally are brave enough to follow our instincts, things have a strange way of working out exactly as they should? Since the dawn of the "Great Homeschool Improvisation," the very same mental health and educational professionals I was so worried about began approaching me and asking me more and more vociferously to share the recipe I was creating at home. Apparently, not only did they *like* it, they *loved* it!

I was flattered, but befuddled. Like many Aspies, I was diagnosed in adulthood secondary to my children's evaluations, and I was still teasing out which parts of my personality and thinking patterns had to do with Asperger's and which didn't. I wasn't really sure what it was about my approach with Asperkids that was so original.

My problem was mindblindness, a classically Aspie tendency to have trouble delineating between one's own thoughts and understanding and other people's.

That's part of what makes it so hard for us to tell you what we are good at, or what we need help understanding – we can't always tell where our knowledge ends and yours begins. My Aspie son asks me what "that" is on the DVD screen, even though it is playing behind my head in the car. I can't see it. But he can, so if he doesn't think about the question first, he still intuits that I can, too. My daughter answered a test question by explaining that no, one couldn't ice skate across the Atlantic Ocean, but perhaps one could cross part of the Arctic Ocean on foot. She was right, but she didn't get credit, because she never explained why the illogical scenario was impossible – that the Atlantic is never solid while part of the Arctic might freeze. She just assumed the knowledge in her head was obvious to everyone.

As we grow up, we Aspies learn to "connect the dots" between our thoughts and our words a little bit better, but it has to be a consciously acquired skill. And even then, it's not easy to delineate what we know versus what everyone else knows. Therein lay my problem. If I was going to make things better for the millions of Asperkids out there (not to mention their families and caregivers), I had to figure out exactly what it was that I, as an Aspie, had to share that the rest of the neurotypical world needed to hear. Perhaps it sounds strange to your ears, but this was a painfully difficult task for me. Even specialists, who worked with spectrum kids constantly, didn't seem to grasp the source of my confusion. I wanted desperately to be the voice for our beloved children, and was being told by professionals I trusted that I could "help to change the way we do so much for these kids." That's a monumental responsibility that I did not want to blow. But to get inside your minds and then be able to ascertain what you need to know from us was almost impossible for me.

I am a teacher and a mom, but I am no curriculum expert, well-paid psychologist or lifelong special educator. So, in a very "typically Aspie" get-to-the-point-without-sugar-coating-it way, I put this question to a close friend, a college professor and herself the mom of a spectrum child; she had been to the same lectures, read most of the same books, learned the same lingo and put a ribbon on the back of her minivan, too. "So why," I asked flatly, "don't *you* know this stuff?" She smiled and said, "I think your question is actually why don't I understand our kids the way that you do?" I nodded. "Because, honey, you are Aspie. I'm not."

Now that made sense. Without a word or hesitation, I "get" my children's Aspie idiosyncrasies. I know them, I feel them, I recognize them. Most of the world doesn't think like these kids think. More often than not, I do. So, I would just tell our story.

There is an expression which says, "If you've met one Aspie, you've met one Aspie." Every person diagnosed with Asperger syndrome is a unique expression of a common family of traits – like siblings who are visibly related, but one has a little bit more of Grandma around the eyes or of Dad in the jaw. One's point on the autism spectrum may look more like classic vanilla ice cream, a "milder" presentation. Another person may be more double fudge chip, a stronger expression. Either way, it's all ice cream, made with varying portions of the same ingredients: "unfiltered" speech, sensory issues, tunnel-vision hyperfocus on some topics and inability to focus on others, rigidity of thought, concrete, literal understanding, need for routine, trouble seeing others' perspectives or integrating their ideas, social anxiety, love of logic, personalization of critique – the list goes on. We are all different – no woman could speak for her entire gender, no Caucasian for his entire race. In the same way, I would never be so arrogant as to say I speak for all Aspies. Even between my own Asperkids I see great natural disparity in temperament and disposition. But there are enough similarities in all of our experiences to warrant a vast overhaul in how the world recognizes, understands, and responds to Asperger syndrome. From the inside out, Aspie has to be reframed.

I am honored to get to share my approach to parenting, teaching, and loving Asperkids. And it occurs to me that, in the crazy road my life has taken, at age 36 I have perhaps finally discovered what it is I want to do when I grow up. On behalf of all our wonderful little people, I want to change how the world understands Asperger's.

Consider this my version of an Aspermom's handbook, then. It is an engaged outlook from within. Ironically, I am part of a group whose main characteristic is that we don't fit into groups. And now it's my goal to get you to fit in a little bit better. My tactics evolve constantly; they will, I imagine, continue to do so. But my "insider's" view never will, nor will the fierce mother-love that will forever guarantee my drive to protect their pursuit of happiness.

Simply put, what I do and say stands upon what I believe. Therefore, what I believe about Asperger's informs every theory and practice in this book. We're not talking clinical definitions or doctoral theses. I offer no pretense of either. Instead, my "life" degree is now 36 years in the making, plus bonus time for years teaching and parenting multiple Asperkids. And that, I'll wager against anything put forth, has got to count for something.

The face of Asperger's

Asperger syndrome, like most profiles, is both for better and for worse. It is a descriptive name for a pattern of skills and challenges which will react similarly to certain environments, curriculums, supports, and situations. And it isn't new. It's a pattern that has only recently been named, and is still widely misunderstood. And yes, there is a trade-off for the mind's terrific creative intensity and unique intelligences, and usually, it manifests as interpersonal difficulties, sometimes leading to anxiety and/or loneliness. But there is much hope, as long as we Aspies can find our way to the careers, teachers, passions and relationships that suit our natural selves. Which is exactly why I wrote this book.

There is no birthmark, lab test or blood work that indicates Asperger syndrome. I can't tell you what it looks like physically, because there is no hallmark. Asperger's doesn't "look" like anything in particular. A syndrome, by definition, is a constellation of tendencies or symptoms, not a disease or illness. So first and foremost, I believe that being Aspie is a phenotype, not a defect. That is, it is the multifaceted expression – neither good nor bad – of a particular genetic sequence. Like red hair. It just is. And more and more popularly, it is being considered by the psychological community to be more of a subculture than a defect.

On that note, a language point. To my family (and many other people), the label "Aspie" seems to feel like a better description than the clinical diagnosis; it communicates, without condescension, a very real set of descriptors about commonalities in the ways we think, behave, and interact. Some of those commonalities are helpful to us, some aren't. But I defy any neurotypical person reading this to be without her own challenges and strengths, talents and shortcomings. "Aspie" is just helpful, non-pejorative shorthand to acknowledge certain patterns that echo among us. Therefore, to avoid the problematic connotations of "less than" which can accompany the admittedly diagnostically appropriate phrase "has Asperger syndrome," I very infrequently either use those words *or* (more importantly) think of myself or my children in those terms.

So, OK, that all said, what are the commonalities among us? Aspies are intense people who see morality, love, friendship, and value in passionately binary terms. It is right or wrong. Someone is a friend or a betrayer. We are loved or despised... even if the rest of the world might disagree with the absolutism of those perceptions. To varying degrees, Aspies can come across as "nerdy" or "geeky," although that isn't a certainty. I remember actually saying to my mom that her lack of help in the wardrobe department had "made me a nerd" (because everything's always Mom's fault!), "but I overcame it." Read in arrogance and self-import, and neither would be accurate. I was unemotionally reporting facts. At one point, I *was* a "nerd." I used language that was intellectually appropriate but situationally inappropriate – honestly, I sounded like a little adult. Grown-ups thought it was adorable, admirable even. Kids – not so much. A big vocabulary doesn't inspire other eight-year-olds, it makes those kids (and some insecure adults) feel badly about themselves. Oh, and it turns out that talking too much was cute only until it crossed the line and sounded desperate. But I promise – no amount of exclusion occurred to me as being my own fault.

Eventually, I had studied (and I do mean that) enough fashion shows and magazines and played enough theatrical roles (always as the vampy redhead) to consciously "pretend to be normal." I had figured out the social rules (more or less) and learned to play by them. And so I welcome you to the first important point to know about Aspies – *natural* social butterflies we are not.

Becoming aware of social boundaries, filtering thoughts, reciprocating in friendships – skills most people pick up without thinking – must be explicated to us or acquired by us through almost academic means (my actual studying of *Seventeen* magazine, for example). Which is exactly how Aspies learn. That is to say that we have to come to understand the world through rules, logic, and cause and effect. After watching social patterns over and over again, Aspies can learn to intellectualize, break down, and then memorize behaviors that neurotypical folks do instinctively. And, of course, put us in a new scenario where one or two details change, and our whole system has to be overhauled. Either way, depending upon one's "acting" skills, the Aspie-trying-to-pass may come across as plausibly eccentric, fly under the radar, or totally mess up and seem awkward, stiff, and insincere. Add that to trouble reading body language (as when someone is edging away from a conversation), perceiving emotions, deciphering facial expressions and literal interpretations of conversation (e.g. when asked "How are you?" a factual answer isn't really the goal), and we can really be in for it.

As has been said, we Aspies have a knack for getting right to the "toenail of the matter." We are famous for missing the big picture and focusing on something totally tangential to the overall situation. It can make for tough times, for sure. But learning to speak neurotypical, or learning to speak Asperger's, can also be seriously funny.

Last week, my five-year-old son achieved a new level of karate belt, and was being presented with his double-orange-stripe in front of a huge crowd as part of a formal ceremony. The problem was that he had worked so hard that he had skipped the entry-level belt – so when handed the higher rank, he began having an in-depth, heartfelt argument with the instructors as to the major problem at hand! Protocol wasn't being followed! From the back of a crowded room, I couldn't hear him, but I could absolutely read the anxiety, rather than pride, which he felt at thwarting the order. Eventually, he turned around with a smile, having been convinced that he'd earned the degree – and let's be honest, it was precociously adorable to see Mr. Mini-Police Officer trying to enforce the rules and keep the adults in line. I realize it's a little less so when he corrects people's grammar, and it really isn't cute coming out of the mouth of a teenager. With help, though, I know he'll sort it out over time. (I have – look how many sentences in this book begin with "and" – I'm such a crazy rule breaker!)

Though I am absolutely alright with who I am, who my kids are, who my husband is, I am not saying that life on the spectrum is easy. It isn't. I wouldn't forfeit my hyperfocus, my intensity, my intelligence or intuition. But what about the rest of it – the tough stuff? Is it worth it? I will be honest. The second important point to understand about Asperger's is that it can be lonely, both for the Aspie and for the family. There are ways to connect – if you know how to find them. We Aspies spend our lives trying to figure out the neurotypical world. Your learning our "language" is your first step in understanding what it's like to be us; then we can all team up for some serious brilliance.

Only one time in my life can I recall an "outsider" hitting the nail on the head in describing the experience. At the Autism/Asperger's Super-Conference I referenced earlier, Tony Attwood drew his presentation to an end with a photograph. In the picture, a group of about ten people in bathing suits sit on the edge of a pier. The day is sunny and bright, the water is glistening, and the group is full of smiling folks, belly laughing and obviously having an absolutely wonderful time together.

But the catch is this: we see the entire gang from the back. Standing maybe 20 feet behind everyone else, we are just beyond the edge of inclusion – a witness, but not a part. Perhaps the happy bunch wants us to join in, politely, maybe even sincerely. Perhaps they don't even notice us. Whatever the case, Tony Attwood finished by telling the crowd that "this" is what being Aspie feels like. He was right. And while everyone feels that feeling from time to time, this is a forever thing – from earliest childhood through adulthood.

Being Aspie means feeling like an outsider, second (or less) choice, so close but yet so very, very far. It is the yearning in a line from the movie, *The Birdcage* (1996), which crept into my soul. Through tears, Dianne Wiest's character pleads to family and strangers alike, "Someone's got to like me best." But even if they do, it is hard to believe it.

Oh, if we were to sit down on that dock's edge, we (especially "Aspergirls," author Rudy Simone's (2010) fabulous term) might skillfully flirt or crack jokes, be winsome and bubbly. Given the right script or role, we can play the part for a while, some of us becoming "social butterflies" for whom making friends seems easy (I was the Social Events *and* Rush/Recruitment chairs for my college sorority chapter!).

Maintaining those friendships is an entirely different story – because it is an entirely different skill. There are scripts, rules, and, most importantly, patterns to follow in establishing relationships – both platonic and romantic. Reciprocity is expected. Thoughts of people and events out of our immediate day-to-day experiences are there, for sure! But our attention is fleeting, and one recollection is quickly replaced by other fast-paced ideas. It's a working memory thing, not a lack of affection.

And if a relationship is established, we may get way too attached; friendly and friend are fuzzy boundaries, confusing and variable with lots of room for embarrassing gaffes. The new person may become a special interest – something on which to happily hyperfocus, though perhaps with preconceived plans for get-togethers, "playdates," or relationship trajectories that don't accurately include the other party's perspective. Then, unable to manage the reciprocity comfortably, or doubtful of the genuine affection we may have won, we may dramatically break off or politely drift away.

My own solution is to be a vicarious friend, or, as a dear friend of mine calls me, a "connector," a term used by author Malcolm Gladwell (2002) in his bestseller, *The Tipping Point*. My girlfriend jokes that wherever she goes, she meets someone who knows me. "You're like Rome," my husband agreed. "All roads lead to Jenny." His case was sealed when, at 7:30 a.m. on a blustery morning in a hotel lobby in Kansas City, Missouri, a Midwestern American city thousands of miles from anywhere I have ever lived, worked, or studied, I ran into someone I knew from university.

My husband and girlfriend are right. And I will secretly admit it's not by chance. It's how I guarantee inclusion on a comfortable level. As a college freshman, I remember consciously finding pleasure in the amount of people who would recognize me and smile or say hi while crossing the campus. I'd engineered it that way. Friends even commented, half-bemusedly, half-annoyed, that they couldn't keep a conversation going with me because of the amount of greetings I'd need to return.

I realize that at first glance, this sounds completely *un*-Aspie. It's not, though. Truth be told, the quantity of pleasantries, rather than the depth of relationships, was what mattered more to me – it was validating to someone who'd often felt left out before. Even today, I feel satisfaction in helping establish positive relationships, and folks appreciate me for the personal connections made, which means they will probably be nice to me, too. I'm like a social matchmaker. It is vicarious success – an illusion of proficiency that keeps me included, though at a safe distance, protected from exclusion or rejection.

So even in our common area of weakness, social skills, there is no "always" for Asperger's. There are, however, patterns of predictable strengths and vulnerabilities you can spot and support. We can muddle through life on our own, stumbling often, battling isolation, low self-esteem (sometimes masquerading as inflated egoism), and school or career indecision. Or, you can help. It takes one to know one, they say. So here I am, ready to help you get to know us.

The plan

Being an Aspie is intense, dynamic, and confusing. The world, as it is, isn't really designed to meet our needs. I can only imagine it's akin to being left-handed and having to try to learn to use right-handed scissors. Or being as tall as a professional basketball player and trying to fit in a regularly sized twin bed. Function and form don't match.

Traditional education is that way for Aspies. Actually, a lot of life's experiences, expectations, and demands are that way for us – just a little bit outside of our comfort zones. Halloween costumes itch. Birthday parties are loud. Casual social get-togethers lack a specific purpose. Adults and children react totally differently to our professorial monologues. White lies are still lies, yet adults excuse them. It's socially alright to break some rules, but not others, and there's no one to tell us which are which. Oh, and when someone asks you how you are, they really don't care! What's that about?

It used to be said to women that it was "a man's world." One could just as easily say that "it's a neurotypical's world" and Aspies are just trying to live in it. In fact, there's even an Aspie website called

"Wrong Planet" (www.wrongplanet.net), as sometimes it does feel as if we are trying to make our way in an environment that isn't quite suited for us. No doubt, your Asperkids feel the same way. It's just one of the many reasons I feel strongly that an Asperger's diagnosis or "label" is a positive thing for anyone (child or adult) to know about, not something to hide. It gives a name to a host of differences of which we are already aware without laying any blame on our part for "failures" or "shortcomings."

This book, then, is your Rosetta Stone. Let me teach you how to speak Asperger's, think Asperger's, play Asperger's. It is my "insider's" advice on how to capture the brilliant young Aspie minds in your life. It's the stuff I wish my own parents and teachers had known, and maybe even what I wish I'd understood better about myself. It's the gift I try (some days more successfully than others) to provide my own children. In a nutshell, we're going to walk through what your Asperkids need you to do for them to make this experience on the "wrong planet" a little less alien.

Harness the power of the special interest

Aspies come with a blaring "access me here" button. You hear it in our conversations (or monologues), see it in our play, and feel it in our tireless desire to stay lost in a world of our own about one particular topic. Whether it be dinosaurs, Greek gods, pioneer girls, or airplane models, an Aspie's special interest is not a perseveration to be endured – it is the most powerful way into our hearts and minds because something about that interest speaks volumes about our own self-concept. In our home, I have taught complicated math patterns with allosaurus and brachiosaurus rubber stamps, and the concept of division using "dino eggs." I have introduced solid figure geometry by building models of the Parthenon, and music theory by compiling Mount Olympus playlists for the iPod. Short and simple: the child's passion is the way to get him passionate about learning.

Visit the show-me state of mind

Aspies are concrete thinkers. By providing a child with substantive items to experience through her body (respectful of sensory sensitivities), she will move toward abstract concepts with a powerful understanding of the why's behind operations, theories, and formulas. Don't tell us. Show us. Grammar can be explored through three-dimensional models, binomial equations through block design, "square roots" through building actual squares of numbers. (Did *you* ever learn that laying five rows of five identical items makes a square shape of 25? I didn't!) Sensorial learning based in tangible beginnings allows the child to understand concretely, and then expand to abstract thoughts in a way that she probably wouldn't otherwise.

Find a detour or seven

Search out or invent ways to feed information to and coax understanding from the child without allowing the physical limitations to hinder him. The truth is that our kids tire easily and frustrate even faster. So, whether it's dyslexia, expressive disorders, obsessive-compulsive disorder (OCD), dysgraphic handwriting, motor planning issues, memory problems, or visual or auditory processing issues (and at our house, my children negotiate *all* of these), get the body out of the way. Employ keyboarding early on, write math equations with rubber numeral stamps, engage the pincer grip and avoid scissors by using a pin-poke (essentially a push-pin stuck in a cork) to trace tiny holes around shapes, puzzle pieces, or animal or geographic outlines, use crayon-rubbing plates to illustrate without coloring, move wooden alphabet letters to practice building words, spelling, or alphabetizing. Provide a creative platform for him to experience real learning, success, and independence before his body stands in the way of his showing you (and himself!) what he knows.

Remember the absent-minded professor

"The absent-minded professor" was my mom's nickname for my dad, and it fit. My dad was a brilliant international litigator, yet at 60 years of age, he managed to flood the kitchen by loading and running the dishwasher with paper plates. Aspie minds are so busy hyperfocusing on the minutiae of the world that we miss a lot of other things. So, be a flowchart for your Aspie. I remember learning somewhere in grade school that there are something like 37 steps to making a peanut butter and jelly sandwich (PB&J). Simplicity is relative. Skills which are obvious (to you) and necessary (for us) to live independent, hygienic, personally and professionally successful lives require structure and systematic instruction. What is basic to you must be broken down and taught to us over time, all the while respecting sometimes fragile egos. Step-by-step clarity, directness, portioned information on how (and why) to manage things both academic and practical (like how to pour without spilling, fold laundry, wash dishes, hang clothing, match conversational volumes, pay bills, maintain the home) are not remedial. They are necessary.

Long story short – it's about respect

It comes down to one sentence: respect the child for exactly who she is, and she will amaze everyone. Don't fear the unexpected. Love unconditionally and let her know how you feel, boldly, proudly, and often. Do everything possible to remind your child that in your arms and by your side, she will never feel rejected. She will only feel valuable and important.

On these points, I speak to you with the authority of one who has grown up with it, lives it, sleeps beside it, and teaches to it. What follows is my guide to what is working here, every day in front of my own eyes, supporting the learning, practical life and social and emotional strengths and challenges of my own Asperkids. I will try to act as interpreter for you and for the kids – mine and maybe yours, too. Of course, no one person can ever speak for an entire group, and in no way do I want to imply that I represent a homogeneous group of all "Aspies." Instead, I offer my own life on the spectrum as an "Aspergirl," married to an Aspie hubby (yup), and now named an

Aspermom of three beautiful little people (one girl, two boys), each with his/her own set of gifts and obstacles. Turn stumbling blocks into stepping stones. It takes one to know one. You get the idea.

We Aspies are big on if/then logic (remember those from back in high school geometry?). If given the reason for something, then I can see the storyline, the inevitable conclusion, the meaning. I will do my best to explain the commonalities I see threading through the ways we think, learn, adapt, and interact, and the original ways of reaching into the spectrum that follow. Necessity is the mother of invention, they say. I guess in this case, it was the needy mother who did the inventing! So, I humbly and hopefully offer you – parents, teachers, and caregivers – the very real, go-to learning strategies, practical life solutions, and social and emotional supports that I have adapted, synthesized, and/or invented in my own teaching and parenting.

Given the right tools, you too can empower, empathize, and embolden, whether that means using my plans verbatim or ingesting them and tweaking them to your own little people's unique needs. Permission granted to use as is. Permission also granted to take liberties and use my work as your jumping-off point. Just take faith in knowing that when you serve their vision in the face of their many adversities, it simply matters that you are present.

That was the case just yesterday for my littlest boy, the one who (finally) got the red hair. Coming in from an errand, I found him throwing a terrible tantrum for his daddy, crying pitifully and hitting himself on the head. The problem was that from sunrise to bedtime (literally), he insists on wearing his Spiderman costume, and, well, Dad wasn't so sure about bringing him to his toddler gym class in Spidey muscleman polyester. The little man has such a tough time there anyway, and doesn't ever want to get involved. But in reconsidering it, Dad came to agree that if our guy needed a little shield between himself and the big ol' world, fine. Who cared? So, we told him he could keep on the suit. Once allowed to head off in costume, he went to the car happily, and had such a triumphant time in class (as Spiderman) that he actually played along with the class for the first time ever. Let the child be himself, and he will amaze everyone.

Lining things up

*Lining things up is an Asperkid's way of making order
out of a big, unpredictable, uncontrollable world. And as
you can see, the finished result is pretty satisfying!*

Redhead. Aspie. Superhero. Whenever the unexpected arrives – and
it will – there is a jolt. A pause. A recentering. But if you think about
it, the surprise isn't really in a label or a name. After all, whatever the
nomenclature, it is clear from the start that she is different, whether
she is a redhead, or an Aspie, or maybe even a superhero in disguise.
No, the surprise is your acceptance, an unexpected hand to hold or a
respectful smile. It is our lot, after all, to be who we are. But oh, how
wonderful it will be to have you share the not-so-typical journey.

2 SPECIAL INTERESTS
The Way In

The "if" part of the statement

Virtually every Aspie has a special interest. While not an exclusive determinant of the diagnosis, I have yet to meet an Aspie who didn't have a topic that fascinated them to no end (and probably bored the living daylights out of their weary audiences). As already stated, I wholeheartedly believe that there is no more effective way to bond with an Aspie child or to support the acquisition of functional living and learning skills than through the almost magical portal of special interests. Through this method, I have found ways to encourage interdisciplinary learning, improve frustration tolerance, facilitate social interaction, and establish an emotional connection with precious Aspie kids.

But before I can explain the "how's" of my theory and methods, I absolutely must take you on a journey with me. As promised, this is where I start bringing you, for maybe the first time, inside the spectrum. Let's call this part the "if" section of a two-step idea; the "then" part will come later when I tell you about what I have done with my own kids, and make suggestions on how you can apply this work in your own home or classroom.

Here's the thing: *if* you are to properly, respectfully, and productively access the special interest as a "way in" to that child's mind and heart, you must understand *why* the interest is so special. It is, to quote my husband, sacred. It is absolutely enmeshed with the individual's sense of self and her life in a neurotypical world. So, to get you to "get" us, I have to take you on a journey with me, and offer you a place to stand by my side. I must ask you to try to step into our Aspie shoes, so that you do not simply intellectually understand, but rather begin to empathically feel the power of the all-too-overlooked access tool you are being offered every day that you spend with your child. Once you begin to "get" where he or she is, you can begin to work your way and draw that child further out. This is our first chance to share the insider's view. But I warn you – it's not always pretty.

The Wicked Witch is dead. And resurrected

You are hereby invited to the Land of Nail Salons, Big Hair, and Pegged Pants – my home at age 12, New Jersey, USA, in 1988. For those not native to the area, let me paint it this way – the TV "home" of the Mafia-boss Tony Soprano on the infamous show *The Sopranos* is located actually in my hometown. Just under an hour's drive from New York City, it is a suburban land of bagel shops and pizzerias, where expectations are high and so are property taxes.

The school year before, seventh grade, had been the worst of my life. I am not honestly sure if there was a single day that I didn't come home and cry. But academically, it had been a breeze.

My Language and Civics teacher, Mrs. Greene, had been very tough – and I *loved* her for it. The more she asked of me, the more I wanted to excel, to be the perfect student for her. Oh! And we'd learned grammar (I know you're gagging now)! Sentence diagramming, word function, breaking down ideas like teasing apart lines of music. As a piece might be dissected into melodies, bars, and notes, suddenly language danced not only in my ears, but also before my eyes. Parts of speech were as quarter or eighth notes, each with its own rhythm; sentences were like musical phrases. They were consistent, mathematical almost. Precise but poetic. Form and function in grammatical pattern.

Right. Not exactly a common reaction to old textbooks asking bored adolescents to pick out the nouns and verbs. I get that. But it was mine.

Life on the other side of the expandable wall, however, was pure hell. There, things were a lot more casual, which for most kids, meant more fun. The Math and Science teacher was a long-term substitute, the mom of a classmate. As an adult now, I can see that she had every best intention, and that her laid-back classroom probably gave a nice foil to the higher-stressed environment in Mrs. Greene's room. I despised every minute.

Casual meant more unexpected moments, opportunities for kids to crack jokes, move around, disturb the safety of teacher-led-lecture or question and answer. As if it were yesterday, I can remember our science class playing a pre-test quiz-bowl. Actually, the idea seemed fun to start. *Jeopardy!* was a favorite quiz game show of mine anyway, and maybe, I thought, I could even win some points for (and favor from) my teammates. The next question went to me, and I answered. I got it wrong.

That shouldn't have been a big deal. But you see, Jenny never got things wrong. If I couldn't be anything else, at least I was as perfect in the classroom as possible. Heck, the gym teacher had me correcting my classmates' written tests so he wouldn't have to, in exchange for "the 100 I know you'll get anyway," and a teacher the year before had had me proofread, edit, and rewrite the other 30 or so students' social studies research, and then write and direct them all in the play on the eighteenth century American Constitutional Convention that followed – yup, these all made me really popular with classmates, as you can imagine.

And now, I'd let everyone down. I'd made a mistake. Not such a big deal in the scheme of the world. As I tell my daughter, that's why pencils come with erasers and keyboards come with delete buttons. But mercy was not mine. From the back left corner of the room, a boy stood up and began to sing, "Ding, dong, the witch is dead!" And he sang the entire "Wicked Witch" song from *The Wizard of Oz* (1939) over and over as he skipped around the entire room, back to his seat. The class roared. The teacher stifled a giggle while shaking her head at him. And that was it. Next question, Team 2.

Some 23 years later, I can still see his shirt untucking as he skipped. I just sat, trying not to cry, expecting someone to make it stop. No one did. I have heard that up to 85 percent of bullying goes unobserved by adults. That is true, I am sure. More often than not, it's much more subtle, quiet, understated. Teachers can be right there in the room or on the playground, and often be totally unaware of the social dynamics playing out in front of them. Years later in a chance meeting, my mom told Mrs. Greene about how bad that year had been for me; the poor woman broke down in tears. She had never known a thing was wrong. And yet, everything had been wrong.

It was also during that year that two girls in my class took it upon themselves to figure a way each afternoon to make me cry. This I know because the nanny of one of them saw me years later in a store and confessed she'd hear them talking nightly on the phone about what to do to me. Although one had worn a "best friend" locket with me only the summer before (remember what I said about making versus maintaining relationships?), now they got their kicks involving the whole class in publicly humiliating me; creating elaborate practical jokes at parties, engineering "fake" boys to call me at home, that kind of thing. And yes, I always fell for it.

I was naive, I was different, and I came over as pretentious and arrogant, I am sure. That's not because I was either pretentious or arrogant. It's just that my intelligence was all I had going for me; it was how I garnered praise. And my theory of mind (TOM – the ability to accurately imagine another's perspective) was so off, that I thought if I tried hard enough and did well enough at everything, kids might like me for the same reasons grown-ups did. After all, parents and teachers frequently asked others to "be more like Jenny" right in front of me. I followed the rules, was polite, and gave every ounce of energy I had to getting things right. And, mindblind as I was, I truly thought that by constantly displaying how smart I was, starring in school shows, *and* making competitive-level athletic teams, I would earn my peers' respect and friendship, too. Didn't quite work out that way. As my mom asked me once, "Why doesn't anyone you want to be friends with want to be friends with you?"

Ouch. Obviously, as perfect as I was trying to be, I was still a total and utter failure.

I remember asking my mom to teach me how to make friends. But back in the 1980s, my mom didn't know what to make of that. "I didn't know how to *teach* someone to have friends," she's told me, looking back. It's not like "social skills" clubs or camps were available at speech therapists' or psychologists' offices as they are today. A "gifted kids'" psychologist she took me to meet once told me just to stop being so difficult for my mother, she was getting very upset. Funny, a therapist who saw my six-year-old daughter said the same thing after meeting her for a single session. "You don't seem like a pushover. Just be sure to show her who's in charge."

Really? It was the same sick feeling I'd had years ago. Authority hadn't been the issue in 1988, and it wasn't the problem in 2009. My son has a T-shirt that says, "Discipline doesn't cure Asperger's. But thanks for your concern." Once, in her second class assignment in six months, our daughter had an in-school meltdown; she was worn out, embarrassed, lonely, and miserable, and that day, she totally lost it – sobbing and screaming outside the classroom, unwilling to go in. In a phone call later that evening, the teacher interrogated us. "I am just wondering," she asked curtly, "if you ever discipline this child?" I thought I might vomit, but my husband spoke calmly into the receiver. "Ma'am," he replied smoothly, "I have been with the police force for over ten years. My father was a colonel in the Marines. If this were a discipline issue, it would've been solved long ago."

In an arrogant tone, one veteran teacher doubted the accuracy of the Asperger's diagnosis (as if it's an easily achieved rubber-stamp); however, when I asked her – thanks to a tactic espoused by Julie Clark, the author of *Asperger's in Pink* (2010) – how many *girls* with Asperger's she had actually taught, she conceded the answer was "none." Like heart attack symptoms in a man versus in a woman, Aspie looks a little different in females. Published voices in the field, like Tony Attwood and Rudy Simone, hope the feminine "variation on a common theme" will become better known. So do I. Because from first-hand experience I can tell you that, just like a heart attack, Asperger's in girls and women is every bit as real and life-altering as for the men and boys we already know.

But back in the moment, the teacher continued to lecture us, observing that yes, our daughter did hold back from groups, but

"I think she's just a lot like you, Mr. O'Toole. You know, hesitant." Hmmm – foreshadowing. This was six months before John's own psychologist diagnosed him with Asperger's. So, maybe the teacher got at least one thing right after all.

Our child was out of that school within the week. I love my husband for holding his ground. I love my child for trying her hardest. And I love that for this generation, we could do better because we knew better.

The truth was that I had no idea what I was doing wrong in seventh grade, and there wasn't much in the way to help me. Fast forward a few decades and my eldest kid wasn't exactly making headway by playing with Barbie as Elphaba (the Wicked Witch's name in *Wicked – the Musical*, her ironic first special interest). Our boy's insistence that *Blue's Clues* be on TV constantly, that all crayons in the house be green striped (as on the show), and that all people and inanimate objects correctly reenact (verbatim) his favorite episodes didn't exactly win friends and influence people either.

While my daughter was still young and physically tiny enough to be considered a "cute novelty" by adults and peers, playdates often ended with her hiding somewhere in the child's house, or with embarrassing mommy exchanges. I remember picking her up once, the mom trying uncomfortably to tell me that they couldn't really follow the storyline of my child's play, and "there wasn't a lot of cooperating going on," when her daughter chimed in, "Mommy, can I *please* have Annie over to play *now*? *She's* finally going home." Smile and nod, usher kid to car, get the heck out of there before she hears this.

Voices like that still haunted me: the older neighborhood boy who followed me home daily after second grade, shouting "Dictionary Brain! Encyclopedia Head!" for everyone to hear. Games were "locked" on the playground, and at seven years of age, I was tired. That was the year Miss Grant read Laura Ingalls Wilder's *Little House in the Big Woods* (1932) to our class. Something about it caught in my heart, and stuck there, to be resurrected again in a few years' time.

At some point in seventh grade, I came down with bronchitis and missed two weeks of school. Sick as I was, it was the best fortnight of the year. If I couldn't figure the "rules" out of how to act during free time after lunch or before school, maybe it's not that surprising that the rules of clauses and participles felt awfully reliable.

And that's why, once summertime came, I wanted to escape. Not just from school, but from the world. Please don't think I was suicidal – absolutely not. But I am sure I was depressed. Aspies are very aware of what we can do well; we are also keenly intuitive as to what we can't. Personally, I felt as if I were a constant embarrassment. My mom, a *very* social person, would tell me to go to the pool, play tennis, call someone and do something.

As if it were that easy for me. My mom, like many parents, figured that if she pushed hard enough socially, I'd finally just figure it out, like I did with everything else. That's about as true as me telling my husband's diabetic pancreas to get over it and start producing insulin again. Biology doesn't change because you tell it to. Or because we want it to.

I had learned long before that year that being alone was easier. You can't make a fool of yourself when there is no one there to watch. And if you can find a version of "alone" that offers escape from the never-ending thinking, then, dear reader, you have a special interest.

In that summer of 1988, I was hoping for an escape that would get me very, very far away – just over a hundred years back. Like a long-lost friend, a memory returned of a place where things were better. I gathered photos, read biographies, memorized timelines and travel routes. For most children who read her books, Laura Ingalls Wilder was a girl in a house on a prairie, back in some vague American pioneer era. I still remember, however, that she was born in February of 1867, that the *Little House on the Prairie* television show was basically hogwash (though, duty bound, I watched every syndicated episode anyway), and that in her very real, historical world, family was everything, everyone belonged and the simplicity of a tin cup or regular weekly chore routine could bring great worth to the life of a young girl. In her recently published book, *The Wilder Life*, Wendy McClure summed it up perfectly. "Who knew how many times those books made me idly wish for a *now* other than the one I was in, that the world would somehow crack open and reveal a simpler life?" (McClure 2011, p.151). An Aspie's special interest is that crack in the world, a route by which she can slip away to "anywhere but here or now," as Tony Attwood said.

Laura's artifacts even offered me her favorite Scripture verses, found beside her bed in a handwritten journal upon her death. In these private notes, it seemed to me that my distant friend was reaching out to help me. Psalm 27, she wrote, was one of her favorites when feeling alone. It spoke of being kept safe from enemies who surround and attack, of feeling special, not condemned, of being protected and loved. It was as if, very much alive somewhere in time, Laura knew I needed her. I can say for certain that my lifelong habit of seeking solace in faith began with what felt like "advice" from my friend, Laura.

I was no fool. I knew full well that I was 12 years old, growing up an only child in late twentieth century suburbia, not a member of the Ingalls clan on the mid to late nineteenth century frontier. But maybe, just maybe, there was a way out. McClure wrote, "Sometimes it felt like there was a trick to it, that if I held this thing [from Wilder's time] long enough I'd somehow be more human than I was now" (McClure 2011, p.184). There was a part of me – a very real, very deep and very powerful part of me – that hoped if I could devour enough names and dates and places, God would send me to a time and a place far away where I truly belonged. Obviously, this wasn't it.

And that is what a special interest is. To those outside the Aspie world, our perseveration on a topic is exhausting. I know: in my job as Mommy, dinner may well include concurrent monologues about Athena, dinosaurs, and Spiderman. Now try making picture-perfect family dinnertime repartee out of that!

But whether it is Spidey, an allosaurus or a debate over the actual color attributed to Athena (gray, not silver, which was Artemis's, I am corrected), to an Aspie, our special interest is the gateway to the world we construct out of facts, fantasy, and logic. As much as you hear, it is only the tip of the iceberg of the wealth of thought, the seduction of belonging, the sacred – yes, sacred – dimension where we cannot mess up or be excluded. Where no one will ever skip and sing in celebration that we are "dead."

The transportive power of a special interest is the first function. It is the one that serves us. But a child's passion can also be made to serve you as a glimpse into what the individual most values, and how he sees his own self measuring up to that yardstick. I invite you to examine the trajectory of special interests a person holds over his or her lifetime. Look for themes. Specific interests may last as white hot, short bursts, or continue to varying intensities over years. But generally, they do evolve.

We may never put away a love entirely, but we move on to another. Let me try to help you relate. You may have had conversations with long-time friends who point out similarities in dating partners you've chosen, maybe physical, maybe personality types, maybe both. Maybe you see trends in types of people you prefer as friends or bosses. Whatever the case, you can step back, take a look at those patterns, and draw some conclusions about yourself. The same is true of an Aspie's special interest; as you read, in my early life and in those of many kids like me, sometimes it is the best friend we have.

My husband recalls his topical fixations rolling generally from tanks to military planes, from knights to Star Wars, Celtic history (he learned Gaelic on Long Island), quantum physics, then animal science. Seems kind of all over the place? Maybe, maybe not. I see a continuous respect for power, authority, timelessness, and conclusive right versus wrong. He was systematically wowed by science which proved his theology, and passionate about honoring the straightforward nobility of cultures past. I heard an equine therapist once say that we do what we need. Order, structure, honor, strength, connection. That's what he did, and to this day, as his best friend, I will promise that's still what he needs to be happy.

Our daughter, as I mentioned, was first fascinated by the Wicked Witch in the movie, *The Wizard of Oz*. Truly, poetic irony to Mama here. Anyway, I don't know about you, but personally, I couldn't stomach the witch or her flying monkeys until I was well into elementary school. She terrified me! But not my little girl. She was drawn to the Wicked Witch at age two when, somehow, she saw her on screen. For a myriad of serious medical issues, we were in and out of hospitals a lot; when a traumatic procedure had to occur and we needed to distract her, the requested DVD was always "Oz, Mommy."

Mind you, it wasn't a dream of a perfect land over the rainbow or ruby slippers that kept her coming back – it was the Witch. At age three, given free post-op choice of any toy in the store, she chose a Lego Duplo set of the Emerald City because it was Lego (obviously) and included the Witch. The following summer, when her dad and I went to see *Wicked: The Untold Story of the Witches of Oz* (2003) on Broadway, she was so enthralled with my descriptions of the plot and music that she literally begged me to pull up bootleg recordings of Elphaba the Witch on YouTube. The soundtrack became background music to our lives; posters decorated her room. That Halloween, when she was four, she dressed up as a witch – if you judged just on outward appearance. But if you asked, you would be flatly told that you were speaking with Elphaba.

That love has never gone away. Last year at seven, I finally took her to see *Wicked*, and she waited after the show for literally every actor to come sign her playbill. For her eighth birthday this spring, we booked a children's theater company where the kids got dressed in full costume and make-up, and put on a song from the show. Guess who was Elphie?

Just over a year ago, I was describing my daughter to a bookstore sales associate. "She *has* to read 'Percy Jackson,'" the gal told me. And she knew what she was talking about. The book series, by Rick Riordan, tells of a young boy who discovers that he is the demigod son of a mortal mother and the Greek god, Poseidon. Percy is a disaster in every school he attends until he is sent to Camp Half-Blood, a summer camp where all the kids are half-mortal children of Olympian gods. We began reading the first installment, and a new passion was born. Since then, our home has been filled with Camp Half-Blood T-shirts, every book on mythology imaginable, and DVR recordings of any and all National Geographic Channel shows on ancient Greek architecture, religion, and culture. Barbies are now Athena and Aphrodite acting out timeless fables, and it probably goes without saying that this past Halloween, our little Elphaba this time hit the trick-or-treat circuit as Athena.

So, what did this tell me about my child? Actually, it wasn't that hard to see if I sat with her "friends" for a while. In *Wicked*, we learn that the villain, the one who is "different," is actually the heroine.

Against all odds, Elphaba will "defy gravity," flying upwards, embracing the awkward witchy "costume" others have assembled for her as they continue to misunderstand her efforts to "do good." From high atop the theater, she sings defiantly to the jeering mob below, rejecting their slanderous name-calling. Elphie is free of their intimidation and condemnation. No. No amount of disdain will topple her.

The characters in the "Percy" series also have to fight to survive where they don't belong. Every demigod at Camp Half-Blood (and many Asperkids) is dyslexic and has attention deficit hyperactivity disorder (ADHD) because they are hardwired for another time and place.

As loud as her little self could yell, as tall as her little body could stand, my daughter was saying that yes, she knew she was different, but that it was because of – not in spite of – her very differences that she was special, that she mattered, that she belonged. And when I told her recently of how I used to wish against all reality that somehow, if I just knew enough, felt enough, wanted enough, I could get to Laura, to the one friend who understood, my own little Aspergirl began to cry. "On Google Earth, I look for the strawberry fields, Mama," she said. I smiled. In her books, strawberry fields camouflaged the mythical Greek camp from mortal eyes; she, too, was hoping that there was a real place where she belonged. She needed the world to know that she was neither wicked nor weird, she was just who she was supposed to be.

And so I spoke in her language. I hugged her and sang a line from *Wicked*, because I knew that nothing would be more potent than her own special interest in letting her know I *got* it. I heard her. Softly I called upon the lyrics of friendship and admiration. She, too, would change the whole world, like Elphie had changed those who truly knew her, "for good."

Using what your Asperkid is telling you: AKA the "then" part of the statement

Now that you have begun to feel how crucial a special interest is to an Aspie, what do you do with it? In other words, you've digested the "if" (my child is Aspie and has a special interest), so now it's time for the "then." Then…what? "This sounds amazing, but how the heck do I do this? Where do I start?" asked one friend of mine. I'll admit – again, I hit a roadblock here. I am, to quote a teacher friend, "hardwired" this way, so the most difficult job for me is breaking down for you a process that feels as instinctive and natural as breathing. Let's give it a whirl, though, and then look at how I have applied the steps in my own home, classroom, and family life.

Step 1 Observe the child engaged in the passion

Is the interest really, say, lawnmowers or Harry Potter in general? Or are there particular aspects of the interest that seem to most pique curiosity and excitement? If a specific character or mechanism is the best of the best, make note of it; it will be your best asset. Look for those themes!

Step 2 Don't be a "poser": know your stuff

OK, I have to give credit for this line to my husband. When we were discussing his interests over the years, his demeanor changed quite suddenly at one point, reflective, I think, of the still-present import the long-past interest held for him. "But you have to know what you're talking about. If someone had tried to talk about tanks, and either not known some of the major terms or been really inaccurate, they'd have lost all credibility, and I would've gotten really mad." Right. Don't be a poser. Don't meet the Pope not knowing much about Jesus, and don't meet a dinosaur-lover telling him all about how you love the brontosaurus. (There is no such thing; it was an archeological error. This we all learned – loudly – from my four-year-old when someone gave him a brontosaurus shirt as a present – awkward!) If you are going to walk the walk, you have to be able to talk (at least some of) the talk. Otherwise, you are a trickster or blasphemer in their eyes.

Step 3 Get creative: the world is a big, fat classroom

Eyes open – look around. The special interest (in this day of information overload) is everywhere, if you just look. Websites (I list my favorites in the Resources section), book stores and libraries, community calendars, cable listings, podcasts, Netflix (on-demand internet streaming video in North America), museums, craft stores, concerts, your very own backyard! Seize that interest anywhere and everywhere and use it to get your child over the humps. Everything is less scary when presented in the scope of the interest. Think about it: a child is rolled into surgery with a stuffed teddy under her arm because a trusted "friend" makes the experience less frightening. Similarly, the Asperkid *can* negotiate and maybe even conquer skills and scenarios if her "security object" (that is, her special interest) is alongside. Your child feels vulnerable in the world, though she may even appear arrogant in her (sometimes well-performed) attempts to disprove that reality.

Learning disorders, social misreads, perfectionism, traumatic memories, impulsivity – they all exacerbate the anxiety Aspies feel about asking questions, admitting confusion, tolerating frustration or making mistakes. Eventually, anyone would feel like there's really no use trying any more. But if the challenge happens under the auspices of a special interest, success (grand or incremental) is much more likely.

One of the main reasons that I chose my undergraduate school, Brown University, was because it encourages students' participation in designing their own curriculum and interdisciplinary studies, and even offers a grade-free pass/fail option to entice students (who, like at most Ivy League places, were *very* grade driven) to experiment in an academic genre that was completely foreign to them.

For example, on my tour of the school, I remember hearing of a class called "Physics for Poets," which tried to lure word-crafters into the intimidating world of quantum physics and astronomy. On the surface, that may sound a bit odd. But really, it was just a wonderful example about what the university held above all: love of learning. And really, if you're not inspired to write by some of those Hubble space telescope photos of the majestic depths of space, what's it going to take? But the point was this: to move the student body out of the restrictive tendencies of perfectionism, and just get them exploring without fear of "messing up." Classes like this took the audience's chosen love (poetry, writing) and connected it safely, creatively, intriguingly to realms of thought, practice, and process that most would never have even considered trying (wormholes, cosmic calculations, and dark matter). Your child's special interest can do the same thing. How?

Well, a love of fish may be stretched to include learning about the chemistry of salt versus fresh water, a close reading (even an audio book) of Ernest Hemingway's *The Old Man and the Sea* (1952), or of the effects of changing environmental restrictions on commercial practices. Listen to "The Downeaster 'Alexa'" by Billy Joel (1990), and examine the lyrics as poetry. Play it on an instrument. Look for an internship at a pet store or with a wildlife fund. Read Native American folk tales on the salmon. Learn the methodical, step-by-step process of catching, cleaning, and preparing a meal. Practice consistent caretaking by earning, purchasing, and then maintaining an aquarium.

Encyclopedic knowledge of American presidents could lead to investigations of one figure who is now believed to be Aspie (Declaration of Independence author, Thomas Jefferson), of what makes effective speechwriting and/or public speaking, or to doing calculations to determine time in office, between various leaders' terms, or their life spans. Learn about their favorite foods and then cook them using authentic-to-the-time recipes found online; play with period toys. Discover the trades some considered, and try to watch the modern versions in action; compare and contrast how those professions have changed over time; or maybe even look at their diplomatic styles, and see how those relate to (or don't!) the social skills we're trying to learn. Map out the birthplaces of each as an exploration of geography.

The possibilities are endless. Read on – you'll see.

The particulars: temples and dinos and superheroes, oh my!

Apparently, the first thing that I did differently that caught the professionals' attention as I took over my children's schooling was that, without giving it much thought, I used what we had going for us. Meaning, of course, our special interests. At our house, that meant Greek mythology and paleontology.

I believe that learning should be global – interconnected. After all, post-graduation we don't operate on a math, then science, then foreign language schedule. Knowledge is connected. So, the acquisition of knowledge should be connected as well. Never mind what wasn't working. We were going to start over by letting the children take the lead, following and filling in until I saw how they would agree to be led.

First, I determined unequivocally that most any special interest can be a bridge to learning about almost any larger subject. I realize that most of you who read this do not have an eight-year-old Aspergirl who loves Greek mythology. I have two other Asperkids, and neither of them is too keen on the subject either. That's OK. Any one special interest-based approach can still work as a case study for teaching or reaching other Asperkids. My husband didn't like school. He remembers being bored out of his wits in math class, and finding it absolutely impossible to stay still enough to listen and learn. "But what if," I asked him the other day, "instead of about comparing apples or oranges, your math problems were about tank parts. And what if you were given the prices to repair various broken gun turrets (with the correct names given!), which you had to add and then compare to the price of a new model tank, in order to advise the government on whether to repair or replace?" Even at 39 years of age, his eyes lit up. "Now that," he smiled, "would've grabbed me."

You may remember reading that my Aspergirl's passion was (and is) author Rick Riordan's series of books about learning-disabled kids who turn out to be the half-blood children of Greek gods and goddesses; they live and train against evil in a secret summer camp called Camp Half-Blood.

My daughter, like her dad did before her, struggles with math. While she understands concepts, as I became her teacher, I saw how multiple learning disorders would layer one upon another until she found that even if she "got" a concept, memory problems, clumsy material manipulation and a host of other challenges made math about the last thing she wanted to do. She'd stall, she'd deflect. She'd rage, call herself stupid, and usually wind up in hysterical tears.

A particular example that jumps readily to mind was in working with the concept of perimeter. First, it's not exactly a blockbuster interest-wise. A little creativity is definitely necessary here, especially with Aspies. Remember the if/then mentality? If we're going to learn something, then you have to tell us why we should bother – why it matters, why it's worth the effort. I remember a book that all the biology majors had to read back in college called *The Selfish Gene* by Richard Dawkins (1976). Mind you, I never did read it myself, but from what I understand, the idea was that all humans are hardwired to behave in ways that benefit the survival of their species or genetic codes. A male spider doesn't mind becoming his lover's lunch, as long as he's had a chance to pass along his genes before mealtime. Whether we're talking spiders or people: make it work for me or my progeny, and I will play along. I am not sure that I agree with that doctrine, but from where we are in our discussion, let's go with it.

As we know, Aspies are, by nature, more egocentric than your average Joe or Jane. It's not that we think we are more valuable, important, unique – insert pompous adjective here. It's just that we have a very, very hard time getting out of our own minds. So, without giving it much thought, I made "perimeter" relate to the main characters in my daughter's favorite books.

First, vocabulary. Why? First, it was a way to make the mathematical concept logical, second, it made it interdisciplinary, third, I could relate it to Greece. I began by teaching my daughter the song I had learned a million years ago as a sorority pledge. Paired with large font examples of the actual Greek letters taught to the protagonists, my little tune was short and simple – plus it made for a funny story of Mommy having to learn the Greek alphabet at some ungodly hour in untold collegiate circumstances.

We messed around with the sounds and built phonemic blends until I brought out the actual words "peri" and "metros" written in Greek. We translated them to English letters, and then talked about the meanings – deciding soon afterwards to begin our own dictionary, adding entries in both alphabets whenever we found a root word, prefix, or suffix that had come from Greek origins (and suddenly we had vocabulary expansion, not to mention the dawning of an understanding of etymology).

OK, so if "peri" meant "around" and "metros" meant "measure," my little detective deciphered "perimeter" to mean the measure around something! But when drawing little squares and rectangles on paper with mini-measurements, it was going to be difficult to manage the fine motor issues, and a whole lot less fun than if we could take the next step outside – making math real.

The Percy Jackson series had sparked questions about Greek architecture. So we went out to the driveway, chalk and measuring tapes in hand, to draw giant aerial views of the Parthenon and the Empire State Building (a battle site in the books), camp cabins and more. Walking around our driveway, my girl did her own measurements, engaging with and internalizing the idea of "perimeter," and then (in giant chalk numbers) did the calculations to boot. Last, with prompting and dialogue, she was able to generalize patterns in the "buildings" she'd measured into formulas for finding the perimeter of a square versus that of a rectangle. Of course, there were moments when I had to redirect her attention or limit her choices when problem-solving. But the fact is that she stayed excited, involved, and positive about math – all because it felt like (and was, actually) an extension of her special interest.

Oh, and how did we work around handwriting? By learning keyboarding beginning at age seven. And guess what she used as practice? That's right – direct copies of pages from her mythology tales and mythology-based novels. Now that's way better than the quick brown fox.

Then there was the day we were broaching the topic of division. Personally, I learned it as a series of number tricks on paper that didn't really mean a whole lot, but I made sure to get right to get my "A."

And that was about it. For my daughter, with a whole lot more going against her learning than I had, it was another case for going Greek.

My preparation involved concocting some stories about the "camp cabins" and new "dining rules." Ahead of time, I had made a fill-in-the-blank chart and then, at lesson time, I began to tell my tale. Due to some fire regulations, the children of the various Greek deities were going to have to be reseated for meals. So, we were going to use some beads to represent campers and help figure out how many tables would be needed as various scenarios arose. She loved it.

What follows is the table I made for her to complete (with my help, of course) on her first day playing with the concept of division (and no, I did *not* ever mention that word until *after* she'd rocked the lesson).

Total # of demigods in cabin	Demigods per table	# of tables	Division equation	Multiplication check
12	4	3	$12 \div 4 = 3$	$3 \times 4 = 12$
64	8			
18	6			
99	9			

For your purposes, this could feature dinosaurs or fish species, train track capacities or troops at Waterloo. The specific subject is irrelevant. The method is what matters because the possibilities were, and are, endless (presently, she's extended her exploration of ancient life to Egypt, so there's a mini-Nile River Delta growing in her bedroom for science and physics, including the building of an ancient irrigation machine, called a shaduf, with natural objects).

Maura as Isis

*Special interests are jumping-off points for learning. What began
for Maura as a special interest in Greek mythology expanded
and eventually inspired learning about the evolution of writing
and math systems (doing work in Greek, Latin, cuneiform, and
hieroglyphics), geometry, etymology, agriculture, and religion. Last
Halloween was Athena, this year, Isis! But always – learning.*

Rubber band temples have been constructed on GeoBoards (math manipulatives usually used to practice plane geometry or build finger strength) – that's spatial planning and geometry. A book report assignment on one of the books from the "Goddess Girls" series (a teenage, high-school version of Athena, Aphrodite, etc. by Holub and Williams 2010) called for the construction of a three-dimensional school locker. The instructions I gave her read:

Athena's Locker: Your book report on *Athena the Brain*

Part 1

Use a visual/graphic organizer to help you summarize the book. It doesn't have to be long, just clear!

Part 2

Design Athena's locker at Mt. Olympus Academy.

1. What color will you paint it?

2. What does she keep inside?
   * Books
   * Special keepsakes
   * Photos
   * Posters
   * Magnets or stickers
   * Lunch
   * After-school supplies for activities/sports/clubs

Creativity, comprehension, written expression – "special-interest-ified." And there's been so much more.

For Christmas, her favorite Greek deity, "Athena," sent her a "summer camp care package" (addressed in Greek). Inside was a bevy of treasures. The International Star Registry had included a (real) "name your own star" kit, as we had begun studying astronomy in more depth, paying specific attention to matching planets and constellations with their equivalent Greek mythological roots. A calendar for the new year linked with all we'd been studying about the evolution and nomenclature of our calendar names – following our modern names for the days and months back through time to their origins on Olympus.

There was a wooden model of the Parthenon to build, and to examine closely, looking at all these new three-dimensional geometric figures – categorizing triangles and prisms in the process. Iris, the goddess of the rainbow, snuck an actual glass prism in the box, too, just to check out the cool ways light could be refracted. There was even a latitude/longitude scavenger hunt to play on Google Earth. By entering the coordinates, my little Greco-phile could follow a series of clues from one landmark to another – navigating the travels of her favorite characters, seeing real-life photographs of the attractions she'd read about, and getting an amazing sense of global geography and mapwork.

But the single best part of the package was the Parthenon playlist that had somehow appeared on Mom's iPod. It was a chance for her to experience that special power music has to help "dance" in someone else's shoes: empathy. From Bananarama's "Venus" onward, it was inspiring, fun, and a deeply meaningful gift. Furthermore, it was a melange of musical genres, styles, and tempos – fodder for great discussions about why one song or another reflected the perspective (theory of mind work!) or feelings of the associated character. Plus we got to boogie around the living room in our socks. Awesome.

Did it matter to her? She never said thank you. But this year, my daughter is finally old enough to take part in an Aspergirl camp offered by a local psychology group. The girls ranged from 8 to 15 – and would you believe it, the eldest girl is a hardcore devotee of all things mythological, specifically the books of Rick Riordan ("He's my idol!") and the ancient Greek tales in general. Despite a seven-year age difference, these two bonded over the minutiae of the stories, the chance to dress in Athenian garb, and to talk to someone who loved these characters on an intimately personal level, too. "I was speechless, then joyful, Mommy," she told me.

Girls in chitons

Special interests can also be a way to make friends. Here, Maura and a friend in Archeology Club are dressed up in homemade chitons.

Initially, she hadn't been too sure about camp; maybe that's putting it nicely. She honestly admitted that she didn't want to spend any time thinking about how "weird" she already felt. But it turned out (thank heavens) that Aspermommy's gut instinct knew what this Asperkid needed. Last night, her daddy asked how she felt being there, among the seven other girls at camp. "Normal," she smiled. "Finally." In the past, she'd reflexively rebelled in the face of self-examination. She'd crawl under tables or into corners. It was just too hard to be the "other." But if she could do that work in her element, with peers who respected the importance of her golden goddess robes, then even feeling "normal" became possible.

As I've mentioned, our middle guy loves dinos. Skill-wise, though he just turned five, he's been ready to read for a long time; but his eyes would fatigue quickly, his attention was so short, and his sensory seeking so great that I had resolved not to even bother pushing the issue. Then, the dino books came, and suddenly, the words were flowing like Jurassic lava.

Remembering that Sean is dyslexic and has ADHD in addition to Asperger's, this is the method by which he (at four years old) readily learned what we call "ten buddies," that is, the single digit addends that combine to form ten. Appealing to his special interest, I cut out scraps of bright yellow paper and stamped dinosaurs on them. Then, Sean had to run around the room, matching quantities and types of dinosaurs, so that if he matched the "plateosaurus" bits, he would always correctly be adding 7 and 3. I also wrote out scraps with the equations $7 + 3 = 10$ and $3 + 7 = 10$, which he would find and place by the correct dino addends. Thus, not only did he learn concrete quantities and their abstract equation equivalents, but also he kinetically absorbed the commutative property of addition: no matter what the order of the addends, the sum is always the same.

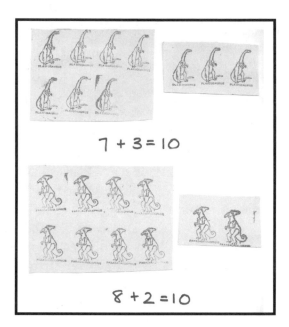

Dino math

What I mean to say is simply that, like his sister, put his learning or skill-building in terms of his special interest, and he will outdo himself. He has worked complex math patterns because he was using dinosaur stamps. Yesterday, we practiced cooperative play and fine motor under the guise of coloring in some dinosaur Shrinky Dinks (flexible plastic sheets that can be colored in, and shrink and harden when baked). We took turns giving directions; he traced, and I colored. Figuring out the oven temperature for our triceratops required a bit of comparative math (adjusting the preset oven temperature), and even figuring out that the two sets of two legs made four altogether. And "Why did the plastic dino get so hard after he shrank?" lead into a review of how molecules behave differently based on temperature.

Today was Dinosaur Day at social skills class (which we just call "playgroup"). Coming off a weekend that included a "roaring" good time at his fifth birthday paleontology party, our little professor showed up to group complete in field hat, with excavation gear and the "fossils" he'd discovered during our birthday dig. Although selective mutism has been a problem for him when anxiety becomes too great, my mini-museum curator apparently rocked the day; he answered questions put to him by each group member, shared without any trouble, and actually enjoyed being the center of attention (not his usual gig). In the frame of reference of his special interest, demands that might otherwise lead to tears instead brought confidence and smiles.

Next is a project I gave my daughter to synthesize her work in geometry, operational math, and ancient history. Best of all, it gave real-world application to the skills she was learning and matched with a History Channel special she'd watched on *Engineering the Impossible* (historical engineering projects like the pyramids, the Coliseum, and Great Wall of China). The first-person letter format engaged her in a more personal way that she really enjoyed, involved her special interest of ancient mythology, and required that she (with help) compose a reply letter containing her calculations, so it also became an opportunity to practice letter-writing.

Dear Ishnefet,

Greetings from Thebes. We send you great regards and warmest wishes as we begin this joint venture to design a new temple for the Great Goddess Hathor.

Below I have inscribed the general layout of the main floor.

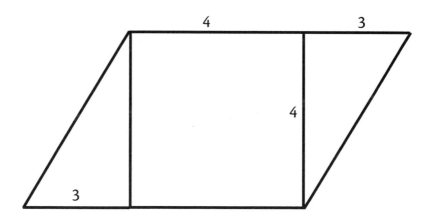

In order to trade for the sufficient lapis and marble floor tiles, we will need to know the temple's perimeter. I have provided the measurements given to me by the local masons, but need for you to fill in remaining distances and calculate.

Next, the center room will be inlaid with gold. Can you tell me the area I must be able to cover in melted metal? At 15 shekels per square of gold, how much money will I need to summon to pay for the gold?

Also, we need to know the area (that is, how many square measures) the two side chambers will cover IN TOTAL. Floor tiling here will cost only nine shekels per square measure. Based on the area you calculate, how much will the temple's side portions cost Pharaoh's treasury?

Last, the sacred Aten sun window (in the shape of the divine Sun Disc) will be divided into equal bands of ten colors — but our glass cutter can only measure by fifths. If we need to cover 4/10 in blood red garnet, how many fifths should I ask the glass cutter to slice?

I look forward to your reply.

Be wary of crocodiles this time of year,

High Priestess Mutaknee

What about your Asperkid? That's where your work comes in.

You see, every child is unique (Aspie or not), every special interest is unique, every family is unique, and every schooling situation is unique. So, it would be totally presumptuous and uncaring of me to assign plug-interest-in-here "prescriptions" for specific activities in various settings for any Asperkid I hadn't met. More than that, a fill-in-the-blank formula would do a major injustice to the child, and maybe even make her feel as though her interest had been violated.

But, here's the key: having journeyed with me back to 1988, having stood by my side as I devoured all things Laura, you've come to better understand the power of the special interest. By closely looking at my husband's and daughter's special interest trends, you've seen how much they reveal about the Aspie in questions. So, "if" this is what special interest means and illustrates, "then" you must give that child his or her best chance at social, academic, and emotional success by using it for the information vehicle it can be. How?

- Observe.

- Know (your stuff).

- Get creative.

By learning how to thoughtfully observe the personality themes your child's interests reveal about him, researching and then creating activities around the special interest of the day, parents become better able to support a love of learning, have positive homework time, instill daily living skills, and face the unknown future together. This is a matter of teaching someone to fish, not handing out a single dinner. Your child's fascination *will* change over time. If I were to write today, "This is how to explode Star Wars into wonderful adventures," what would you do when suddenly "Twilight" or model trains take over?

You would observe, know your stuff, and get creative again. And again.

Whether the special interest is fish, superheroes, Star Wars, ancient Egypt, Littlest Pet Shop, Harry Potter, no matter. The charge for those who love the child is first to understand the role that special interest plays and never, ever degrade it – to the Asperkid, if you insult his interest as weird or boring, you are directly calling him the same things. Look for what that passion tells you about the child, what it is that she needs, wants, values, and how she thinks she measures up against those ideals. Learn as much as you possibly can about the special interest. Then, *use* it. You *can* do this. You can connect the *Titanic* to newspaper reporting and writing skills. You can link bugs to animal classifications and botany. You can tie model airplane building to the physics of flight and military history. Turn a passion for horses to real-life experiences in agriculture or getting better readings on body language.

Besides being a mommy, in what seems a past life, I had the great honor of being the teacher to several classes of wonderful middle schoolers with some distinct learning challenges. On paper, I had no business being there. My background wasn't in special ed, and I was a lateral entry hire (meaning that I was earning my master's of education while actively teaching). Giving no thought to interoffice politics (that's mindblindness, not nobility of character speaking), I focused every ounce of love and creativity for my students. Apparently, though, I was doing something right; in my first year of teaching, I was nominated for Disney's American Teacher of the Year Award. In hindsight, I think it was really my "street creds" that were informing my work.

More than a decade later, I recall one student who struggled with multiple learning issues. He despised reading most everything presented to him, acted out in class, and never really invested in anything he did. But I noticed that every time he walked in the room, he had a magazine on dirt biking tucked into his slipping pile of school supplies. Without knowing the term "special interest" (it was 2001, I still hadn't even heard of Asperger's), my instinct was to seize this entry point to a child I was otherwise losing.

So, we had a little meeting one afternoon, during which I told him that he was allowed, if he so chose, to log his magazine reading time for credit, write article summaries instead of book reports, and make clear, well-developed and researched, informative presentations on the topic to his classmates. "Really?" he asked incredulously. "I mean seriously?"

Yup, seriously. And at the end of the year, his test scores (oh, I can't stand those things but still) were all dramatically improved, his attention was better in every way, and his work was funny and complete. "I will never forget you for this," I remember him saying. "Thank you."

He wasn't a spectrum kid, and I am not some amazing wave-a-wand-and-change-the-world educator. My point in retelling his story is that I also understand the strict parameters under which teachers operate. Faced with multiple classes of 20-plus kids each, limited resources, and defined class periods, it is not easy to individualize curriculum to students' special interests in the ways some of our brightest instructors would choose to do. But I can say, offering this case as a real-life example, that with dedication, creativity, and keen observation, it is not impossible. Caring teachers "differentiate" their lesson plans every day, and squeaky wheels get the oil. Bring these ideas to your child's teachers and administrators as you also look for ways to infuse them into the home or therapeutic environments. Everyone, but most especially your Asperkid, will be infinitely glad for it.

Remember above all that your child is unique and precious, as are the million and one yet undiscovered ways to harness that passion. We Aspies are never alone when we are immersed in our interests, never bored, never sad. As such, the essence of the interest should remain ours to manage – whether we use it to escape, cope, collect, entertain. Don't let it get hijacked by anyone's good intentions.

But I promise, there is no better way to let a child know she is loved for exactly who she is, or that he *is* actually more capable at math or reading or sharing or staying on task or following directions *if* you build upon a love that is already an intimate part of him. When traveling, are we not always advised to learn some of the local language, some of the customs? It says to the natives, "I value who you are and what you have here." The same is true of learning the words, names, stories, and facts that are the language and customs of your Asperkid's special interest. Taking the time to invent ways to connect, communicate, educate, and love through that "language" is the most effective, encouraging, powerful gift you can offer your little professors, too.

3 ALL ASPIES ARE FROM MISSOURI
Concrete Minds

In the United States, each of the 50 states has a nickname that is supposed to reveal something about the people's character or the region's history. Arizona is the Grand Canyon State, for its famous natural wonder. On the southern coast, Florida is the Sunshine State. And smack dab in the center of the country is Missouri, the Show-Me State. The motto is a bit odd, and of course, we Aspies are not really all from Missouri. But there is something that we apparently have in common with their state slogan. You have to show us, rather than tell us, to get at the potential within.

Ideas that Aspies build on observable realities are often inspired. Sometimes, they are nothing short of genius. Heck, even Albert Einstein (who was very likely an Aspie) came up with his paradigm-shifting theory of relativity while riding a Bern streetcar and pondering the very real workings of a very real clock tower. Other times, it's a little more down-to-earth: using malleable clay and tinted water to show why a peninsula is the exact opposite of a gulf. That's only the beginning, though. Without knowing it, you may have just sparked the interest of the world's next greatest geophysicist or Martian explorer.

The thing is that we Aspies need tangible beginnings to root ourselves in complete understanding of abstract ideas. Let's call it yet another "if" statement: "if" we are to learn concepts rather than memorize facts, elevate thinking rather than replicate theories, interacting with physical, perceptible things is what gives Aspies the best chance to move beyond mere information collecting to higher-level problem-solving and critical thinking. Using material objects to instill basic truths *shows* us why something is so, rather than simply *telling* us that it is so; in doing so, a foundation for (sometimes genius-level) abstract thought is laid.

Think of the old biblical words about a house built on sand; when contrary forces come to pass, the building falls "with a crash." But the one built upon rock – let's call it "concrete" for our purposes – stands tall. Now allow "concrete" to mean something which is real or actual, rather than merely existing in thought or idea. Ideas, like grains of sand, are transitory and malleable. Observable fact is, well, fact. It is comfortable, reassuring, and indisputable. It just is. Therefore, a "house" or concept built upon that fact will be more enduring, too. You see, we Aspies cannot only get abstract ideas; we can sometimes elevate those notions to unfathomed heights. But to own the initial idea, we need that "concrete" rock foundation first.

The human brain learns first through sensorial experience. Neurologically, our mind develops by taking information in through the body. Babies can't conduct conversations with their parents, but they can feel the snug hold of a carrier sling, respond to the bass lull of white noise, or see predictable, familiar faces. Then, they draw conclusions about what creates the feeling of "calm" or "safety" (evidenced by their anxiety and crying when those factors are removed). Really, if you think about it, that's quite an advanced deduction to make. An abstract idea – security/tranquility – derived from tangible experiences.

Back in that summer of 1988, my mom and grandfather rewarded my Little House learnings with an expedition to the Heartland to see the Laura Ingalls Wilder Museum and Homestead. We flew from the East Coast to the Midwest – to Missouri's capital city of St. Louis. Then, we made our way to tiny, rural Mansfield, Missouri. There, hours into the countryside and a century into the past, an elderly Laura had once sat at her desk in a lovely farmhouse. In simple orange drugstore notebooks, she had recorded the story of her pioneer youth.

That such a grand trip was even offered to me was quite a gift, really. Looking back, I can gratefully see where my belief in pursuing one's passions was nurtured that August.

But back to Missouri. My maternal grandfather, a World War II veteran, was an American trivia buff. During the long trip, he had taken it upon himself to educate me on the topic of state nicknames and mottoes. And somewhere along some dusty road along some endless prairie, I remember reading the state-issued license plates on the local cars driving by. "Missouri: the Show-Me State," they all said. It meant a belief in common sense, my grandfather explained. I was intrigued. A lover of flowery language (oh, *Anne of Green Gables*, how you made my heart sing), there was still something oddly appealing about this "show me" thing that stuck firmly in my mind.

One explanation, I later learned, tells of a Missouri congressman, Willard Vandermier. The legend goes that during a late nineteenth century speech, he proclaimed, "I come from a country that raises corn and cotton…and frothy eloquence neither convinces nor satisfies me. I'm from Missouri, and you have got to show me." So there.

Not long ago, I was watching a television show that featured Dr. Temple Grandin, the well-known autistic professor whose work changed the way the world began to understand the spectrum. Asked about her area of interest – animal science – she spoke eloquently, intelligently, and insightfully for an extended period of time. But then an interviewer asked her to define "happiness." Quickly, she became flustered and frustrated. "That's too abstract," she protested. Topic over.

While those two stories seem woefully unrelated, I would argue that they are profoundly connected. Aspies don't like "frothy eloquence" unless it can be backed up with concrete reality. Our minds don't operate on vague intangibilities; yes, we are smart (by definition), and so of course, we can intellectually grasp and explain abstract concepts. But, to really ingest, taste, and then elevate a concept, we are all from Missouri. Don't tell me. Show me.

OK, so how can teachers or parents do that? There are lots of ways to do it well, and quite a few ways to do it poorly. So before exploring the "then," the methods that I've used, invented, or fused, let me better explain the Aspie way of learning as I see it "from the inside out."

As I began to write this book, my daughter asked about the red-hair analogy she had spied on the first page. I explained that I had been getting at the idea of how being different can feel. Grown-ups had a word, "marginalized," and, oh gee, how to explain this to an eight-year-old. "OK, so think of the word 'margin,'" I said, expecting to have to talk about blank parts of a paper and then maybe go from there, but from the back seat of the car we rode in, a little voice interrupted me casually, as she looked out the car window. "Like a leaf."

Huh? "Margin," she replied, "like of a leaf."

Ohmigoodness, yes! The month before, I had begun teaching my children about botany, using mainly Montessori materials because of their sensorial basis for learning. For clear understanding, all children need the concrete before the abstract – this is especially true, and often extended for Asperkids. Eventually, our lessons had evolved into advanced naming and classification; but we started with hands-on activities – going outside and collecting examples from nature, planting our own vegetable garden, and then moving to scientifically accurate, wooden puzzles of the parts of animals, insects, and plants.

One of the botanical words the kids learned was "margin," the exterior edge of any leaf. And though it was far from my mind, when I said "margin" she recalled touching the smooth wooden leaf puzzles, tracing the veins and limits of real, discovered leaves with her fingers, feeling how the crayon dipped when she did paper rubbings of differently sized and shaped leaves. Yes, instantly, she understood that "margin" meant "an outer boundary" from tangible experiences, not from regurgitating a vocabulary word.

Smiling secretly, I pushed her. "Right, like of a leaf. So, if that's what 'margin' means, how do you think someone who is 'marginalized' feels?" Split second pause. "At the edge. Not included. On the outside."

YES!! From a concrete botany lesson, this little child had just applied her understanding to a totally different genre (psychology), been able to accurately hypothesize the meaning of a word *and* intellectualize as to what the feelings of another person might be. I practically danced in my seat. "You are such a good thinker, Sweetheart," I sang out. "Great job making those connections. You rock." And to tell you the truth, I'm not sure which of us was more proud.

Playing with concrete: how to support your Asperkid's version of play

Without realizing it, parents of Asperkids see their children's preferences for concrete thought very early on in the way their child plays. Or, more accurately, they will worriedly note the ways he doesn't play. Where is the pretend? What about my child who finds his own corner at playgroups? Of course, to be able to function in a neurotypical world, we Aspies have to "assimilate" ourselves in some ways. And, by necessity, with support and guidance, we will. But it won't be natural or easy. So, from the start, the ways we interact with the world will look a little different.

Physicians, psychologists, and educational professionals agree that the importance of play in a child's development cannot be understated. Play is a child's first experience of work, learning, and emotional response. Through play, a child practices interpersonal connections, motor planning, confidence in her body, listening and conversational skills, cognitive and memory work. So, when parents or teachers perceive a child to be lacking imagination or problematically preferring solitary play, it is understandable why concern arises.

I think, though, that a little bit more understanding of the Aspie mindset could shift the description of Asperkids' play from defective to different. It all goes back to that concrete versus abstract issue.

My mom recalls that I would frequently ask for playdates – my kids do, too. Aspies do not want to be hermits! In fact, from my own observations, one of the characteristics that set Aspies apart from other folks on the spectrum is how keenly we are aware of our gaffes when trying to be social. While other kids may want to spend hours playing ball or dress-up, our tolerance will probably be shorter – and our true preference of activities lies elsewhere. Group play requires significant cooperative skills, real-time flexible thinking, and otherwise sticky interpersonal play that can feel awkward, uncomfortable, or even truly scary (why Aspies of all ages so often also suffer from social anxiety disorder).

People are unpredictable – kids especially (another reason why Asperkids usually do better with adults). Even if we can figure out how to join in and get along with the crowd, the group environment can assault our senses; by the end, we're stressed, tired, and probably feeling less than confident about ourselves. It's no wonder that retreat to a binary, if/then, black/white, clear-cut world offers respite and relief. That's also why we so often choose to enjoy our time alone or with one well-known, predictable person. Yes, of course, sometimes Asperkids withdraw because they feel (or are) excluded or sad. And that's absolutely awful. But alone doesn't always mean lonely.

Naturally, well-meaning neurotypical parents who see their child alone or playing differently than the rest of a group may recall their own experiences of having been "left out." And so, they will understand their Asperkid's solitary play as forever being a sad thing. Let me offer this peace of mind: it isn't. Sometimes, playing with the kinds of toys we want (less "abstract/imaginative" and more "real") in the ways that we want (without the stress of social anxiety), is the most peaceful time we have.

Think about it from our perspective: if a toy or activity has too many variables, be they interpersonal or progression of plot, where is the fun for us? Our concrete-seeking minds crave clarity and predictability. When most of our day is spent negotiating a world that doesn't match our neurological hardwiring, it is no wonder that we find calm in objects and activities that simplify things as much as possible. Look in a thesaurus for a synonym for "predictable" and you will see "humdrum, boring." That's a neurotypical understanding for sure. It's not wrong, but it's not ours. A more Aspie-aligned version of "predictable" would mean "knowable, understood, not surprising." That means we are a whole lot likely not to mess it up. If we don't "do it wrong," but instead find success in our play, we feel good about ourselves, and are able to develop our learning to higher levels of complexity. Isn't that what any parent would want for her child?

As someone who loves an Asperkid, this understanding should first affect the way that you depict and value your child's manner of play. I have heard, "She has no imagination," from more than one parent describing their child (either disparagingly or woefully). But from where I stand, as an Aspergirl and mom to three Asperkids, I could not disagree more.

An Aspie's imagination will show itself in grand leaps of logic, intertopical connections, and creative problem-solving. I'd like to think that maybe the apparently unique strategies in this book are just such an example of the fruit of an Aspie's imagination. And heck – at one point, I even baked and designed couture cakes! Creativity in buttercream! The issue is merely that we start our engagement of the world (through play) differently than other children; it's not defective, it's not bad, it's just different.

So what's the "then" part of this preference for concrete play? It may be as simple as entering a toy store or searching out catalogs or websites that will feed the trajectory of the Aspie child's play development, rather than shopping for the playthings that the neurotypical parent would have wanted. Toward that end, I've compiled a list of some of my favorite sources in the Resources section at the end of the book.

The first rule in gift-giving is always to think of the recipient. Rather than being forlorn that a beautiful (and maybe expensive) dollhouse or other "pretending" game remains largely untouched, parents ought to try to step into the mind of the Asperkid. What might he or she find most satisfying? Until the Asperkid tries it, you won't know for sure.

My daughter is a lot like I was as a child; as is frequent with Aspergirls, in particular, our toys didn't look too different from other girls'. Back in the 1980s, my collection of Smurfs was enviable. Her litany of Littlest Pet Shop animals was impressive (and knowledgeable – "Mom, did you know that Fluffy's favorite drink is pink lemonade?"). We both had dolls and heaps of stuffed animals, although the inventive story-play wasn't ever really our thing. My Barbies lined up and were posed for photography (with a real camera) in imitation of my mother's wedding album; my daughter would use hers to reenact (verbatim) favorite animated movies. What might (and apparently did, to some adults) appear to be original play was actually scripted, mimicked. But that's OK; after all, children learn through copying, too. Given enough scripts properly applied, you'd be amazed how well we can "pass."

As a little one, my Aspergirl would ask me to "tell me a story from your mouth," which translated to "make something up." I couldn't. Seriously. I would think about it, and always came up blank – oddly reminiscent of days when my own mom would make up lengthy tales about Cabbage Patch Kid adventures, while my dad's bedtime story was the life cycle of a tomato. Less than satisfying on the listening end, I'll admit, but I see now where he struggled. An important caveat, though: my Asperguy, my hubby, never really had the same problems making up stories for the kids. And his army men, he promises, always had some kind of cool plan going, back in the day. Yet he does admit that most of his storylines were based on/in facts, real experiences, or subjects he knew well, and concurs that his thinking instantly gravitates to logical binary tendencies and a willingness to consider theory or conjecture only if it is based in observable fact.

So let's restate this uber-important point: no two Aspies are completely alike – we have common threads among us, but individuals' skill sets are, obviously, distinct. No woman could authoritatively speak for all of her sex. No Caucasian could represent all members of his race. Absolutely no group is entirely homogeneous. The same is true with Aspies. We are not a monolith. We are people.

OK, back to playtime. Until I told her recently, my mother never knew that I'd always found my friends' building blocks to be really fascinating. I clearly remember feeling their wooden planes and wishing I could imagine up some fantastic building to design. But, I never could. So, I'd just put them down and move on. I learned later (while struggling to perfect the art of advanced essay-writing from too-vague instructions) that Aspies first need a tangible, observable model to study and copy. We are excellent at detecting patterns. Give us some models first – not to copy, but to examine. Once we've mastered the patterns within the original examples, we can own the method and be as creative (if not more so) as anyone else.

Just like the Barbie scripts my daughter used, a building plan would have changed everything for me with those blocks. I needed a guide to follow. But I never learned that neatly interlocking construction pieces, complete with step-by-step guides, were readily available at any toy store – in the Lego aisle. I didn't know that kind of toy existed. So, I never asked.

That's why, when I signed my eight-year-old daughter up for Robotics Camp this summer, my mother was surprised. "Really? Robots?" she'd puzzled. Sure, she understood the appeal of Harry Potter Camp, acting, Sewing for Your American Girl doll, but engineering? Admittedly, this child had never built a robot in her life, nor had she asked to do so. So, why now?

Over the years, I've consciously tried to expose her to as many different experiences (and thus, people) as I could. Some things would, I figured, be preferred over others; like me, she found great pleasure in the creative arts. Dance was part of my life for more than 20 years, and musical theatre changed my life. You can't imagine what a starring role in our high school production of the Broadway musical *Damn Yankees* – that involved a striptease and getting "Whatever Lola Wants" (1955) – did for my social life in the matter of one weekend. Or, maybe you can. Choreography, songs, and scripts provide a powerful venue for us to transcend ourselves. Stealthily, we are practicing body language, intonation, and interactions in guided ways that can be "coached" by a director or teacher, rather than "corrected" by peers after a playground blunder.

Like the "eccentric" world of academia, or the highly structured, clearly delineated ranks of the military, the arts, in general, are actually filled with Aspies. Music may transport us as fantasy literature can, or perhaps it facilitates emotional connections in ways we find otherwise inexpressible. Painters, poets, musicians, comics, and writers (widely accepted examples include Andy Warhol, Ludwig van Beethoven, Emily Dickinson, Andy Kaufman, and Herman Melville) are as likely to be Aspies as are generals, scientists, or university professors. We are ever so creative in our own time, on our own trajectory. The beginnings may simply look a little bit different. Aspie and author Michael John Carley (2008, p.14) wrote, "varying degrees of inability toward imagination and creative thinking...may be indications of a great technical mind." Or, they may be the pouring of the concrete foundation upon which our creations can elevate the higher-level emotional functionality of all people.

And so my choices of musical theatre, drama, and the like for my daughter weren't that unexpected. But with Robotics Camp, I was making a very conscious choice – an educated guess. Having learned in the last few years that both my daughter and I were "Aspergirls," I have spent a lot of time "metacognating." That is, thinking about how we think. "If" we think in such an unique way, preferring concrete, ordered information before branching to abstraction, "then" it follows that certain activities will naturally feel comfortable: that meant giving them a chance even if she didn't know (or I hadn't known previously) to seek them out. So I made the deliberate decision to clear out the beautiful but underused plastic kitchenette, and bring very different toys into the playroom: circuit kits, Lego sets, and logic games. And guess what? All three of my kids *love* them – even the two-year-old. And Robotics Camp? My child is beaming with pride over her ability to finally generalize certain academic skills, tackle entirely new problem-solving challenges, and just make some really awesome stuff. Aside from her Aspergirl Camp, it has been the biggest hit of the summer.

By exposing these children to methods of play that innately match their neurological make-up, we give them early experiences of success, confidence, and road signs toward fulfilling, productive careers. Temple Grandin says that her work gave her life meaning. I have to say that sharing this story in a way that may help families better understand and support their Asperkids would do the same for mine. Tony Attwood has found through his research that we Aspies have the largest disconnect between our intellectual ability and career levels; underemployment is rampant. Frequently, we acquire degree after degree, but fall on our faces in the work world – largely, I think, because we have not been guided towards the arenas in which we are simply more likely to succeed.

Let's take yours truly as case in point. Two years after my college graduation, I began the master's program in social work at Columbia University in New York. Department chairs were lauding my papers, A-plusses were everywhere, and within weeks, I was being asked to consider entering the doctoral program. Instead, by semester's end, I ended up dropping out. Classwork was wonderful – I could intellectualize until the cows came home. But the practicum – the social interactions in office or administrative environments – was awful. In hindsight, I should have switched to a graduate program focused on research, intellectualism, and teaching. I would have been content, energized and, I daresay, probably darned good at what I did.

Instead, where did I head next? Everyone said I was bubbly and outgoing (Yes! Aren't I good at putting on that face?!), so, my well-meaning mom aimed me toward the worst of the worst for Aspies – advertising (in client services) and public relations. Disaster. Press releases I could whip out. But beyond that, for Pete's sake, the job description demanded handling the emotional whims of clients, sensing their concerns before they did, and reading every unspoken word in a board room. Could there *be* a more non-Aspie-appropriate career choice? But I didn't have that self-awareness yet. Flashing a pretty smile, boasting a winning educational pedigree, and projecting those social scripts on point, I was hired right away. And dreaded every minute afterwards – misreading my own job performance so profoundly that, six months later, when I went in to ask for a raise, I was told I was being let go because the clients didn't feel I "understood them," and that I didn't really fit in with the other super-social firm employees. Ding, dong, the witch is dead – emotional tailspin, depression, and acute anorexia followed (a hallmark of rigid, perfectionistic, good/bad thinking, often considered a major Asperger's red flag in girls).

No matter how good a performer I was, no matter how smart or flirtatious or eloquent I was, in my own eyes, I had messed up. Without ever having heard of Asperger's, I had no understanding of how I could be so off, such a failure. As so many years ago, when I was clueless as to what about me was so "wrong," now at 24 and just married, I was again lost, confused, and depressed. Michael John Carley (2008) writes that it's in "the nine-to-five office job, where we slip on the most banana peels. Because in these environments the social rules are always the most complicated, they're never explained, and they're different in each office" (Carley 2008, p.12). You're telling me.

I can't promise that any Asperkid – mine or yours – won't go through some of those same pitfalls. I wish I could, but we fight an uphill battle out there. I do think, though, that by starting them out right, in the kinds of play that will most naturally match their aptitudes, we give them the blessing of present happiness and future success.

So, even if your Asperkid hasn't expressed an interest in any of the following playthings, I implore you to experiment and expand her repertoire – she can't ask for that about which she doesn't know. Not everything will be a home run, of course. And be aware that elements of a toy may make a certain item too frustrating, even if the general concept intrigues. We'll talk more about this issue in the chapter "Detours – This Way." But for now, just think about timers (anxiety producing for many children), motor planning, fine motor skills, sensory defensiveness or visual perceptual problems, and how to get around them. Can you get a little creative, make a change here or there? Substitute an hourglass full of sand for a loud electronic timer? Limit the parts of a project into smaller tasks? Where there's a will, there's a way. For example, my middle boy (who is five) likes the idea of Lego a lot – but his hand strength is quite weak, and his eyes too jumpy right now to make the process enjoyable. That's OK, he can still participate when his siblings play; he helps his big sister or little brother sort pieces, or adds decorative stickers to his dad's constructions. In due time, he will be able to do it all. The same thing was true of his sister a few years back, and now she's building the White House.

Seeing how shapes fit together is more challenging for dyslexic kids like my son, but is really important in the development of their visual processing and problem-solving skills. It also directly relates to the Aspie's tendency to miss the larger point over smaller details.

After lots (and lots) of searching for toys he'd stick with, we finally discovered a magnetic tangram puzzle, which enabled him to enjoy an otherwise arduous task. The pieces stayed put, eliminating one frustration, allowed him to focus his efforts and (finally) feel confident in himself. Detours. They may be necessary, but they will get our kids where they need to be.

Tangram

By now you should have a better grasp of how your child's mind works and why he or she may find concrete-based play so satisfying. The "then" part of your job is to seek experiences that will be gratifying, encouraging, and *fun* as your Asperkid understands it. Consider technology (get thee to the app store – my kids swear that everything is more fun if computers are involved), toys, kits, and books that have the following:

- Finite beginnings and endings (Lego sets, wooden puzzles, or those that can be completed by dragging pieces across touch screens, baskets of small containers that open/close in various manners – hide prizes inside!, mazes, brain teasers, sorting games, tangrams, recipe cards, scavenger hunts, analogies, pattern games).

- Catalogued collections (Yu-Gi-Oh!, aircrafts, Littlest Pets, Harry Potter, dinosaurs, insects, superheroes, Star Wars characters, coins, ancient gods, breeds of dogs, rocks/minerals, royal families – anything that would be featured in an "Encyclopedia of…" type of book).

- Clear visual guidelines and intricately engineered parts (building sets, rocket launchers, trains and tracks, rugs with printed roadways, marble runs, wheeled toys, gear sets, circuitry, microscope kits, musical instruments).

- Stories, costumes, toys, games based in real/plausible science or history (Star Wars, American Girl historical doll and book sets, ancient civilizations).

- Accurate, miniature representations of real-world systems (model-building of planes, buildings, cars, planets, archeological digs).

- *Real* child-sized cooking, woodshop, gardening and housekeeping tools – rather than "pretend versions" (to be explored later in Chapter 5, but generally based on the principle that real tools place greater value on children's "work," and engender self-respect and responsibility).

Playing should be fun. Yes, it's important and functional and all those other high-falutin' things, but it is, after all, *play*. As Asperkids, fun isn't always a natural feeling. Heck, being a kid doesn't even feel quite right to many of us. Personally, I couldn't stand it. And maybe part of the reason for that is that the ways I found pleasure in life were "off," or "weird." Weird to you, that is. To me, escaping into the world of a book and away from a million chances to feel badly about myself wasn't weird – it was salvation. And so, the notions of satisfying and enjoyable are a lot more familiar than "fun." Like happiness, fun is transitory and abstract. Above it all, I would take content and effective any day (again – you would never see this from the outside – social chair and former party planner here!). But this is an Aspie reality. Think of it as a "come as you are" party; by meeting that Asperkid where he is, rather than where another child might be, you bless him with the chance to have a personally satisfying life full of purpose, meaning, and yes, maybe even his own version of fun.

Concrete communication: solid words

Temple Grandin's breakthrough book, *Thinking in Pictures* (1996), firmly explained the power of visual imagery in the way many spectrum folks process information. Hearing her speak in person, I will forever remember smiling as she described her mind as a "Google bank of images": when asked to conceptualize, in abstract, the idea of "door," she would, instead, recall myriads of doors she'd seen over her lifetime. Again: concrete as the route to abstract.

A variation on that theme, when asked to think of a "light" or a "child" or some nonspecific thing, notion, or person, I see the abstract idea of thing as represented by the actual, concrete word – the letters "l-i-g-h-t" or "c-h-i-l-d."

Written words are my visual cues. They are, while more abstract than images, my visual anchor to communication. Oral interactions, which demand spontaneity, often leave us feeling rushed, anxious, and (perfectionists that we are) without closure. Never a conversation is left that I don't spend undue time analyzing and reanalyzing what I did or didn't say. Dialogues happen too fast for me. Often, I think I've gotten the gist of things, only to realize that I've totally missed the forest for the trees, hyperfocused on the details of some transient point in the dialogue (that's especially true in group situations). That has derailed me both personally and professionally.

Printed words make concrete things out of abstract ideas. Like many Aspergirls in particular, I was (and am) hyperlexic: that is, I read vastly more quickly than others, absorb what I am reading, and learned to read overnight without tutelage. Phonics, if I must tell the truth, made no sense to me, and seemed utterly pointless; my kindergarten teacher, well aware of a genius-level IQ, was frustrated at why I couldn't (or wouldn't) read as I entered kindergarten at age four. But then one day, as my mother tells it, she and I were driving along when she spontaneously asked, "What does that sign say, Jenny?" She doesn't remember why she asked, in retrospect – but she does remember what happened next. I read the entire road sign from beginning to end, then turned to look out another window without a care. Stupefied, she asked again – picking another unfamiliar sign. And again, I read the whole thing.

Contrarily, the very worst method of communication of all for Aspies is the telephone; we tend to interrupt more and have *no* visual cues to read. My longest friendships have been with friends who have, along the line, realized that I vastly prefer to email or text – that not returning calls does not reflect a lack of value for them as people; instead, it's quite the opposite. Without the frame of reference of whatever body language or facial expression that I can (however deficiently) garner from in-person verbal exchanges, a disembodied phone voice leaves me almost completely lost.

But text can replace all of that. The written word – notes, emails, social media, texting – is the most highly recommended form of communication for Aspies, because it is *visual*, unambiguous, clear, and most importantly, infinitely revisable. It feels good, safe. Delete buttons and emoticons enable Aspies to deliver an idea before we are (so easily) distracted and lose it. We can reread, edit, and rework phrasing. We can start over completely. But most importantly, it is all there to *see* – to perceive concretely, sensorially. Via written illustrations or shared photos, we can "show" rather than tell – anyone who "thinks in pictures" knows that is a good thing.

On the other hand, various self-help books addressed to Aspies make it clear that many of us have a hard time judging "how much is too much" as our "intensity barometers" (my words) are askew, and our lines between "levels of acquaintances" both personal and professional are often nonexistent. Realizing our gaffes (or having them pointed out) is profoundly, painfully embarrassing, as we hate to be so socially clumsy. We've not meant to be egocentric or overwhelming. Still, "paved with good intentions" and all, we often sabotage our best efforts to be informative or endearing.

I remember one of my daughter's teachers asking for "all the information you can share" about her various health and/or learning issues. Being a literal thinker as we Aspies are, I sent it *all*. We're talking probably scores of messages – later, I was publicly chastised by the teacher and her administrator for my overwhelming bombardment of information. I was lost: as far as I knew, I'd done exactly as I was told to do. Note to self: when someone says they want to know "everything," they really don't. Another social lesson learned *ex post facto* – at 33 years of age.

Parents of young Aspies can prevent such pitfalls by discussing online, email, and texting etiquette *before* interaction begins, so as to avoid any discomfort by either party (and as we know, Aspies love rules). That helps a lot. Similarly, older Aspies are recommended to ask their support professionals (therapists, social skills counselors, employers, teachers) for their assistance in monitoring interactions, such as when to cut down on length or content of emails by giving suggestions on how better to communicate so as to prevent saturation and engender empathy rather than hostility.

Regardless of the potential for pitfalls, I encourage you to view written communication as the "concrete version" of conversation. Be it poetry, prose, personal notes, whatever, the written word is a more tangible, malleable version of the spoken word. And for the relationship between you and your child, that Asperkid and his/her peers, teachers, and (later) employers, the rule should be ask, ask, and ask some more about expectations, progress, status, plans, events, and emotions, but give the chance for that dialogue to take place in writing.

My grandfather used to say that "words that are spoken are thin as air, but words that are written are always there." That's true – no one will print out, to our detriment, a transcription of a casual personal or phone conversation. But that same conversation will be over before the Aspie has had good time to process what has actually transpired. And yes, written words are immortal (for better or worse), but at least for us Aspies, they are our most secure form of feeling some level of comfort and control in the concrete weight of emotion and ideas – the most abstract concepts known to humankind.

A bird in the hand: concrete
foundations for learning

I have worn a lot of hats in my relatively short life. I'm an Aspie, was the product of public schools, have been a public school teacher, am the spouse of an Asperguy who attended public and parochial schools, am the parent of Asperkids, have been parent of kids (both undiagnosed, and then diagnosed) who attended private schools, and now am a homeschooling mother. Perspectives, I have. And, as we get to the topic of concrete learning tools, I realize that each reader will bring his or her own situation to the table.

School teachers may not have the resources to purchase extra or different supplies. Parents may feel ill equipped to teach, or that education isn't really their responsibility. This section of the book, more particularly than previous ones, is a call-out to any and all adults who have Asperkids in their world. Teachers: it will be your charge to creatively construct teaching materials like those I will describe, or to explain to administrators or supervisors why dollars spent on purchasing and training could dramatically improve one of the largest growing special education populations in the nation.

Similarly, parents – you are your child's first teachers. You help with homework already, and often, you are seeking just the right tutor or supplements to help your child better absorb that which is going on in class. In the Resources section, I list some of the most helpful websites and other resources for finding effective, tangible teaching tools, and developing lesson plans to use them. It is said, once you know better, you do better. You already know better now what your child needs and why she needs it; so if she is not being taught in the concrete ways which best match her Aspie mindset (no matter whether her grades are stellar or poor), it becomes your charge to advocate that she receives it. Her future will be markedly better or worse for the presence or lack of that advocacy.

Let me show you what I mean.

It's 1981, and we are back in New Jersey. This time, I am in first grade, and it's a busy day in elementary school. Sometime as math began, I was pulled out of class to attend violin lessons – just the way things ran in our tiny suburban school, and my teacher really didn't give it much thought. Whatever she was planning on teaching me and the other little boy in my math group, she knew I would just knock out easily at home that night.

But when I sat down to my math problem, panic rose in my chest. My face flushed, my heart raced and hot tears sprang to my eyes. I had no idea how to do this!

37 − 8?

What? How do you take 8 away from 7? The next one was just the same. And the next and the one after that! In my little life, I had never felt such complete terror. Apparently, I had missed the lesson on "borrowing," or "regrouping," as it is called today.

Moments later, I ran to my mother, who showed me what to do to get the right answer. Cross out this number, make it one less, add a one over here, now subtract. Over and over I copied that pattern of steps: cross out, one less, add one, subtract. And yes, I got them all correct. Whew. But, did I really understand what I was doing – that in doing all of this crossing and switching, units or tens or hundreds were being exchanged, equal in value but different in arrangement? No way. I just knew what number tricks to do to get the answers right.

Algebra – eighth grade, middle school. OK, actually, I loved algebra. It was easy – patterns again. Plug and chug. Like a rhythm, there was no vaguery, just follow the formula. Easy A. But if you'd asked me why a binomial squared worked out as it did, I'd have probably answered "because my teacher says so." That's regurgitation, not comprehension.

When geometry hit the next year, math was hard for the first time. These theorems didn't apply to anything I'd recognized; these illustrated angles and shapes were not reflective of anything I'd experienced. There were just laws and corollaries and none of it seemed based in reality. I made it work, as they say, but my confidence and interest in math were shot. Forget this. There would never be further consideration of some of the science fields I'd wondered about pursuing in later life. I'd do what I had to do to get the grades I needed, but lost was the pleasure of learning and the desire to go beyond. We Aspies are usually perfectionists, and if I was going to possibly be wrong, I was not doing this.

Why was it hard? It was all abstract. I had no real concrete understanding of the most basic concepts, so there was no chance of me taking them further. Years later, in yet another graduate program (education), I discovered the Montessori method of education – and was powerfully drawn to it. I couldn't say exactly why, but there seemed something amazingly tantalizing about the solid materials being used to teach everything from complex math (to little children!) to reading to biology. No meaningless posters or worksheets: there were mysterious *things* to touch, feel, smell, and see. And they all *meant* something.

This, I thought, is how I want my kids to experience learning. Developed by a pediatrician (Dr. Maria Montessori), it is a respectful, child-centered method of education that seeks to respond to naturally occurring stages of physical and psychological development. She coined the phrase "an absorbent mind" to describe the universal ways in which children literally soak up the world around them, first and foremost through their senses (Montessori 1949). Writes Michael Duffy, a Montessori classroom teacher, in his book, *Math Works*, "One of the most basic principles of Montessori mathematics is that students always learn new concepts with concrete materials… materials [that] are designed to lead your child step by step from the most concrete representation to pure abstraction" (Duffy 2008, p.9). That's right – we're talking using tangible materials to stimulate higher-level thought; it's great for any child, but absolutely essential for Aspies.

Oh, but nothing's quite that easy, is it?

Years later, when my little girl was first diagnosed with sensory processing disorder (just a step along the way to Aspie), I was told by every professional I met that, unfortunately, my desire to send her to a Montessori school was not in her best interest. They were right – at that point in her life.

In a vacuum, I believe the Montessori curriculum and approach are ideally matched to the Aspie mind, but without care or intentional regard for an Asperkid's particular sensitivities (like access to an outdoor swing, headphones, or a quiet retreat), the busy environment itself can be about as Aspie-friendly as that ad agency was for me. Quiet and peace is expected – a child who is fearful, bored, clingy, unable to concentrate, or noisy may be deemed to have a "weak character" with "poor interaction" compared to that of a "normalized child." Careful choices by Montessori schools *can* make it an ideal learning situation for Asperkids, if they choose. However, without a nonjudgmental understanding of "his normal," no Aspie kid would stand a chance.

Also, a great emphasis is placed on the power of collaborative learning. Of course, for neurotypical kids with neurotypically developing interpersonal skills, that is super. But Aspies are never going to be particularly successful team players. We're just not meant to be; and while social skills do have to be developed to some degree just to function in the world, linking our concept of self or of personal worth to how well we function in the group is like judging the square peg for not fitting through the round hole. Yes, social survival skills are necessary, of course. If you were to move to France, you would have to learn to speak French, even if you still chose to converse in English within your own home. Similarly, Aspies must learn good manners and basic social skills in order to survive in the neurotypical world around them. But it will never be entirely comfortable.

Thus, to force your Aspie into a situation where, as Michael Duffy (2008, p.40) writes, they are to successfully "interact with others all day long…and to collaborate" is like trying to force a left-handed person to use her right hand. There are serious psychosocial costs when we go against a person's natural hardwiring, rather than accepting and valuing him for the unique talents and gifts he possesses. Yes, teamwork is very achievable for Aspies, but most usually in situations where each player has a distinct role and the end result is not dependent upon negotiations of responsibility or project outcome. If an Asperkid's understanding of his own accomplishment is tied into his ability to negotiate, problem-solve, and produce in groups, he will never feel like a success, as all his energy will be focused on the anxiety of the group-work, rather than on the lesson at hand. Writes Duffy (2008, p.6), "if your child does not enjoy self-esteem [or] is in an emotional state over a disagreement…it is almost impossible for him to concentrate on an academic task." And so what has he learned in the end?

Last, a Montessori classroom is self-directed and always has a lot going on: in one corner, kids are pouring water from pitchers, in another they are laying long rows of colorful beads across the floor, in another they are carrying and then tracing metal insets, and in another they are doing huge floor puzzles or playing bells. Every one of those activities is beautiful, worthwhile, and appealing. But that's the problem. For some Asperkids struggling with executive function troubles – organization, inattention, impulsivity – they are *too* appealing. My son can't remember to tie his shoe if the television is on. Attention deficits are real problems for Asperkids; unless, of course, we are hyperfocused on a task, in which case confusion or aggravation will ensue the moment the child is called away. An Asperkid may have trouble thinking about or completing a whole lot if too much is going on at once.

And because the Montessori classroom is bustling with visual, auditory, and kinetic stimuli, instructors must take special care to give Asperkids avenues to escape sensory overload or seek calming input whenever necessary and without negative consequence. Indeed, when my daughter initially visited the lovely local Montessori school she now attends (some years later), she left the classroom in tears. At that time, the supportive parameters she needed were just not in place yet, nor was the administrative atmosphere welcoming to the prospect of including an Asperkid. And to be fair, she wasn't particularly emotionally stable at that point anyway. "It was just too much, Mommy," she sniffled. And you know what? For the time being, she was right.

So for now, Montessori school was out. But once I was thrown headfirst into the homeschooling world, I remembered my love for the materials. After doing some research, I finally understood that what I loved so was the concrete, sensorial basis for establishing real comprehension of abstract concepts. Montessori educator Lesley Britton (1992) writes:

> A young child reaches the stage of abstraction gradually, but first he must have *experience* of the physical world, followed by learning the *language* to describe the experience. Finally he learns the *symbol* – the word or number – which represents it. (Britton 1992, p.33; emphasis in original)

Though the process is true for any child, for Aspies, "actual and factual" is a lifelong preference.

I had a discussion today with my daughter as we sat down to explore a new math concept. "You know," I began, pointing to a group of numbers and equations, "all these squiggles are really just made-up labels. Math is actually real." She looked at me, perplexed. And so I began to explain how math was, indeed, very real; that quantities and the ways they interact had been around long before someone bothered to name them, much less make up some arbitrary squiggles to represent them.

For instance, as I touched her eyes gently, people have always had "this many" eyes, right? She nodded. At some point, someone called "this many" by a sound: dos, or due, or two. Someone else, somewhere else, decided to make a mark on clay or stone or papyrus that stood for the sound, which stood for the quantity. Maybe it was II or β or 2. But whatever the written label – or equation or sentence of labels – it was just a substitute for a very real, touchable, observable, concrete thing: the amount of eyes she had. Numbers and equations and formulas aren't actually about squiggles or markings; math is reality. If we can observe the reality first, then we can use numbers just as we use letters and words and sentences to describe a real flower or a real rainbow.

"A rose by any other name would smell as sweet," Shakespeare wrote. True. Speak "rosa" in Latin or "loke'ula'ula" in Hawaiian, or write the letters "r-ó-s" in Gaelic, and we are all using abstract sounds and squiggles to signify the real, concrete thing – an actual flower. The Cherokee nation, my daughter has learned, was one of the few Native American groups who had their own syllabary, or written recording of the sounds in their language. But, I asked her, does that mean that other tribes – like the Inuit – couldn't speak of whales? Or that the Mohawk couldn't sing of battles? Of course not. Without writing, words still exist; without words, things and ideas still exist.

Similarly, without numbers, equations or formulas – like the binomial expressions she was about to learn – quantities still interact. Single cells still divide and multiply. Hours of daylight still wax and wane. Abstractions, labels, describe interactions that have always been true.

And so, we went on to use manipulatives to experiment with the ways in which two quantities being combined (called binomials and written as $4 + 5$ or $a + b$) acted when they occurred repeatedly (multiplied). We used real beads, observed patterns, and then concluded that we could use squiggly labels (numbers) to describe the very real ways those quantities always behaved. We laid out two beads next to three beads four times over and called it $4 \times (2 + 3)$. Then, we played around, and found that we could make a switch and just lay out five beads four times, calling it and writing it $4 \times (5)$. Or, we could combine four sets of two beads with the four sets of three beads, and describe it as $(4 \times 2) + (4 \times 3)$. Either way, the reality was the same – a concrete observation that we could call "twenty" and label "20."

Asperkids need concrete to precede abstract, reality to precede pictorial, language or numerical labels, because that is exactly what happens in the real world. There was one moon orbiting our planet long before we named that quantity or decided on how to write the count. There was water flowing eons before some early human referred to it by a sound, and then later by a series of characters or hieroglyphs. Asperkids' preference for concrete foundations is completely logical. It is how reality operates. And for good measure, Asperkids seem to need to reacquaint themselves from time to time with the reality and tangibility behind abstract ideas in order to retain them.

An Asperkid adores extended and repeated three-dimensional, physical, sensorial learning experiences; when provided with tangible tools to make those experiences possible, complicated concepts become much more readily understood and applied in critical-thinking situations. His "mind is fed...the way he is able to handle and move them around, the discoveries he makes from that manipulation...the self-correcting [nature of the materials], and the geometric visualization he gets to reinforce his abstract understanding" (Duffy 2008, p.45) are so much more engaging and effective than traditional worksheets, textbooks or (ick!) flashcards. As an Aspie, that just makes sense to me, too.

So whether intended to forge a true grasp of mathematics, science, history, geography, or language, Montessori materials quickly became the favorites in working with my children. I went shopping – online and in catalogs – and did literally hundreds of hours of reading on how to properly use what I acquired. And, while

I do not expect another parent or educator to invest the same time or resources, what I discovered was profound.

Let's talk numbers

Remember that story about my meltdown after missing the lesson on borrowing? The truth is that even once I was doing it – for years – I didn't really know why. I just knew to cross out and add a one elsewhere. My daughter, too, had learned to "regroup" in school, but she had no idea why she was doing what she was doing. It was time to bring in the new "toys."

We began by playing a game I called "Pay Day." I showed her small golden beads, tiny representations of the concept of a unit. These little things, I learned, helped establish "a concrete understanding of the decimal system, [and were] the first and most concrete Montessori tool for teaching [a child] to add, subtract, multiply and divide whole numbers" (Duffy 2008, p.11). Indeed, my little one could run her hands through them, pour them, line them up. But whatever she did, they were really little, and that made an impression. It was supposed to.

Next were ten beads strung together on short wire, called ten-bars. On a floor mat, we made a column of ten loose unit beads and brought up one ten-bar. Indeed, her eyes showed her that ten units seemed to take up as much space as a single group of ten. Then we brought in a balance. The ten-bar went on one side, and bead by bead, she counted ten units onto the other. Yes, as our joints and muscles could feel, and the scale confirmed, ten units weighed the same as the single set of ten, too.

On and on we went. We would again get down on the floor, but now with the pearlescent, golden ten-bars. Since ten units had made a single ten-bar, I prompted, let's see what would happen if we put together ten ten-bars. Lo and behold, when she arranged the ten wired rods one next to another, they formed a perfect square. With her eyes and fingers guiding her, my Aspergirl deduced, "Wow, so ten tens makes a square." Thus, the bridge for "squared numbers" and square roots was laid, purely incidentally. How many people – kids or adults, Aspies or not – ever learn that 7×7 or 3×3 or 10×10 is called a "square" because, when we are dealing with the physical reality of math, not the abstract concept of squiggles and superscripts on a page, an actual square is formed by the units within?

The visual and physical comparisons continued once we had counted all of the beads in front of us. Next was the "hundred square," a flat square made up of ten golden ten-bars wired together. She could feel the heaviness of one hundred of something versus ten of that same quantity versus a single unit of it. And yes, you guessed it, the following level was a cube built of ten hundred squares piled one on top of the other (and yes – there is the basis for the discussion of ten "cubed").

Next, I played her a song from an audio math CD I'd discovered in which the chorus repeats "trade 'em in, trade 'em in when you get to ten..." Even the four-year-old got in on the action. And so we sang and were silly. But it made sense to both children: you could actually "trade them in." So, I dubbed one the banker and one the worker. The worker came to me (the boss) for ten units of pay, but when asked to carry all those crazy little beads around the room, had a hard time keeping them together. So, she went to the banker – and, you guessed it, made an even swap of those ten little beads for a single nice ten-bar. They did this backwards and forwards for all of the values and simply loved it. Little did they know, though, that they had just learned the reality behind the decimal system – a beautiful realization this summer on a trip to the Museum of Natural History in New York City, where the planetarium is laid out in a room-sized trip up and down the powers of ten to astronomical dimensions and subatomic proportions. And this little child understood it because of beads.

What about that regrouping thing? When asked to "build" twenty-one, she would select two ten-bars and one unit bead. Next to that would be a wooden chip labeled "20" and a smaller "1" to place over the zero. If seven units (represented by the abstract "7" chip) were to be taken away, of course she couldn't physically do that since there weren't enough loose beads on the mat. Any other ideas? "Yes! I could trade you one ten-bar for ten units! Then, there are eleven unit beads, and I can take seven away from those." In other words, she had just regrouped – not by scratching out the "2" without knowing why, but because the concrete realities in front of her dictated that she apply the knowledge she'd previously gained through sensorial exploration (that ten units equals one group of ten) to solve the problem herself. And she did.

Similarly, this process could be used to solve equations into the tens of thousands (or beyond, if I had the closet space) – once the idea had been mastered, it didn't matter how big the quantity. Only after the concrete work could be executed consistently would I bring in the "labels" – wooden numeral tiles that had to actively be put together just as the manipulatives had been. In layers, the number 5,243 would be constructed from the ground up by adding decimal level tiles: the 5,000 tile for the thousands place went down first. It would be overlaid with the 200 tile for the hundreds place, then the 40 tile for the tens, and last, the 3 tile for the units). After working concurrently with real quantities and labels, eventually she moved entirely to digits only. But working exclusively with the abstract (a digit indicating a tangible amount in her mind) only happened once I was certain she *knew* what was happening and why.

Eventually, these skills would be generalized to plastic chips labeled "1" (always green), "10" (always blue), and so on. The bridge from building and manipulating quantities with countable beads was slowly extending to building and manipulating those quantities with labels – thus an addition problem of 1,243 + 2,132 could be physically constructed out of the appropriate labels: one thousand chip, two hundred chips, four ten chips and three unit chips plus two thousand chips, one hundred chip, three ten chips and two units. Combine all of the above and there are three thousand chips, three hundred chips, seven ten chips and five unit chips, which the student translates to 3,375. These materials are easier to manage in size than the beads, and "move your child one step toward abstraction while maintaining a very concrete representation of the addition process" (Duffy 2008, p.12).

From the basics, the concepts get more and more amazing. The process moves, as the child is ready, to work on an abacus, beadboards, checkerboards, and all other manner of unique tools that successfully urge the child beyond merely arriving at the correct answer, to sincerely absorbing the "why's" of the mathematical processes and encouraging her to explore creatively.

Though a one-time "math-o-phobe," as this year drew to a close, my daughter built on the concrete foundation we were establishing enough to figure out the rule of ascending squares. I was amazed, I must admit – and so was she.

You see, I gave her three three-bars (wired bars of three beads only). How many were in the three square? Nine, of course. Hmm, I wondered, how could we turn that three square into a four-square? Well, first we added another three-bar. Nope, that was a rectangle. But we could lay another three-bar horizontally at the bottom…and hey! That only left one unit spot to fill in, and we'd made 16 – a square of four beads by four beads! She tried it again, building with sevens, threes, fives; each time she saw that a number (later, she'll call it an integer) squared plus two more of itself plus one equals the square of the next number (integer) – $(3 \times 3) + (2 \times 3) + 1 = 16$ and so on. This by the kid who, only a few months earlier, had been successfully regrouping with no real understanding of the equations.

Sensorial block puzzles will soon lead us to complex calculations like bi- and trinomial cubes (algebra), connecting the "geometrical representations and mathematical calculation…embedded in Montessori math materials" (Duffy 2008, p.45).

That method can begin with the very young. When our two-year-old plays with the "pink tower" of ten wooden stacking blocks, they offer him proprioceptive and visual exploration of comparative quantities. Gravity helps, too. Try to stack them in the wrong order and you get a *very* tangible result. Play around some more, and we observe that the bottom block sure feels and looks different than the top one. And so he learns the vocabulary to match the sensations of big versus small, or gradations – there are eight bigger and smaller than's to contrast between the endpoint superlatives.

When the five-year-old uses the tower, he's challenged to look at a two-dimensional representation (an abstract depiction) of a particular block arrangement. He has to try to select and match various sized pink cubes to their two-dimensional representations – something he finds very hard. Then, he has to analyze exactly how the blocks need to be laid out on the ground so that they make the same pattern as in the picture; we always talk it out. Are corners touching? Which ones? Does that go to the right or to the left? The blocks are actually concrete representations of the numbers 1–10, and the tower is, really, a vertical number line. After playing with the tower for some weeks, I asked him to count the blocks, and then he matched a corresponding number to each, with the smallest block receiving the label "1" and so on. After struggling with but finally conquering one particular layout in which he'd had to arrange the blocks in a corner-to-corner alternating pattern, he stepped back and examined the results before him. "Mom," he said quizzically. "Look. I just noticed. All the odd numbers are on one side, and all the evens are on the other. Cool." And back the blocks went on their base. Yeah, I'd agree. That is pretty cool, kiddo.

Special Asper-needs

I was seeing over and over that, though the environment of a Montessori school would not work for my Asperkids, taken into a more Aspie-friendly setting, the materials worked wonderfully for really ingraining the concrete realities of quantitative concepts. But we were running into a stumbling block with my daughter. Although she had been practicing basic addition and subtraction facts for four years and could demonstrate that she understood the concepts, her accuracy without manipulatives was very poor – maybe 40–50 percent. Sometimes the issue was attention deficits. But more often, she just couldn't seem to remember the facts. At her very last school, her teacher made the kids do timed drills each day, and the anxiety that spilled over at home from the teacher calling her "lazy" or "careless" made our daughter sick and her parents furious.

The fact was that we'd sung songs, practiced on the abacus, used every Montessori concrete tool there was, bought iPad and smart phone apps (specialized programs for mobile technology), and any other thing I could dream up. Nothing helped, and daily math work was becoming dreaded by both of us.

Rote memory through flashcards and worksheets is not learning. Period. It is simply memorization. And I appreciate that Montessori and other philosophies like it place so little emphasis on fact regurgitation. Explains Duffy (2008, p.19), "We learned tables first, and then we applied them to problems; in Montessori, your child learned the process first and then memorizes her tables to make her work quicker." Indeed, a typically developing brain will, after repeated exposure, eventually remember that $3 + 5 = 8$ and $15 - 9 = 6$ without forcing the issue. The brain of an Aspie – including fact recall and working memory – doesn't develop the way a neurotypical child's does; frequently, though we can remember other information beyond what seems humanly plausible, we "just can't make it stick," as Aspie teen Luke Jackson (2002) wrote. Indeed, when four years had gone by and my daughter, despite her best efforts, still couldn't remember those basic math truths, we needed to adapt a little bit. She was so ready to move on to bigger and better (and way more interesting) stuff, but was permanently held back by the simple inability to remember.

So, as I had adapted the materials I liked to the environment we needed, I now adapted the method to the child. Once concrete tools have enabled the Asperkid to "own" an idea, it may be necessary to employ additional tactics to ensure he can access the information he has mastered. Then, he will be able to move on appropriately to higher-level thinking challenges.

My daughter could easily come up with "$7 + 6 = 13$" if she had manipulatives, but, absent tangibles, she'd usually resort to fingers. In other words, she needed an ever-present way to keep the quantity visible, not just the digit representing it. Hmmmm…a neat system I'd seen briefly years before, called TouchMath (see Resources), actually superimposed "touchpoints" on each digit from 1 to 9, the amount of which corresponded to the value of the number. So, the digit "1" was written with a single dot on the number where the child was to "touch" and say "one," and so on. A simple addition equation of $7 + 6$ (abstract because it is written only as numbers, or "labels"), then, could suddenly become concrete. Now, the written digits actually contained the quantities they represented. A "7" had seven places to touch, and a "6" had six. So, the addition problem becomes (spoken aloud while touching the points), "seven, touch eight-nine-ten-eleven-twelve-thirteen. Seven plus six equals thirteen." Simple subtraction, multiplication and even division facts are all made more memorable using the system.

But, I cannot emphasize enough, it is absolutely integral that an Asperkid uses a closet-full of manipulatives prior to memory aides, which are then brought out again every time a concept is introduced or reviewed. After a while, the child should be challenged to teach the idea back. Don't tell me you get it, *show* me. For Aspies, real understanding has to be based on a concrete foundation. Otherwise, the joy of "light bulb moments" is missing and, even worse, there will be a point where, like I did, even the brightest Asperkids will eliminate possibilities from their own life plans because suddenly "plug and chug" without deeper comprehension and engagement just isn't good enough.

That being said, in this case, we had firmly established for a very long time that this particular Aspergirl understood the conceptual work at hand. We just needed a way to support the memory when only abstraction (in this case, a number) was in view. And this was it. After a quick trip to the craft store, I'd bought four-inch high three-dimensional wooden numbers, painted them, and glued on buttons for touchpoints – great reminders for her on how to count them, and a fun introduction for my sons. In written work, I could mark out the points if she was struggling, and eventually, she could "touch" without there being any actual points on the page. From an accuracy rate of about 50 percent, she skyrocketed to 90–100 percent in just a matter of one month.

Grammar, physics, phonics – yes, it can be fun

Beyond math, Aspies' need for concrete learning experiences still stands. The possibilities are endless. Physics doesn't have to be confusing (as it was for me). Explore the movement of sound waves in action by striking a tuning fork, touching it to water, and actually *see* and feel sound, as well as hearing it. After experimenting with the properties of gases, liquids, and solids, how they respond to physical forces, stresses, friction, and temperature changes, we made a trip to a transportation museum. There, the Asperkids played with working models of a lock system. And the next thing I knew, owing it all to those kitchen experiments, we were explaining why it was so much easier to move the loads over water than over land to a whole group of fascinated kids. By appealing to the natural way Asperkids need (and want) to learn, we'd been able to extend their thinking and pique their curiosity about the world around them.

Our five-year-old Asperkid gained a fantastic grasp of phonetic work, not by looking at letters but by holding actual physical objects. Remember the order: experience, language, label. Into a large glass storage jar, I piled a plastic cherry, a model stegosaurus, some small wooden steps, a dollhouse chair, a chocolate bar, a postage stamp, some beautifully carved baby chicks, and the stem piece of the leaf puzzle.

First, my little man just got to pull the objects out of the jar; examining actual, tangible miniatures was both delightful and intriguing for him, capturing his attention fully (which is no small feat!). He would turn each piece around and around, inspecting and discovering. Then we began to name each item, emphasizing the initial sound blend and eventually walking around the room, sorting the objects into piles according to their beginnings. Chair, cherry, chicks, and chocolate were placed together. Steps, stegosaurus, stem, and stamp made a group.

The next day, I showed him cards (about the size of playing cards) bearing the letters s, c, h, and t cut out of sandpaper. By allowing him to trace the letter shapes (three times each – and on lots of occasions), the little guy gets repetitive sensorial emphasis of the abstract concept of writing. My Asperboy could feel the curves and straight lines, hear the individual sounds they made, and then physically construct the consonant blends by moving the sandpaper "s" ("ssss") and "t" ("tuh") closer and closer together until he had constructed and was saying "st." I handed him the pre-made "st" and "ch" labels so that he could (proudly) check his own work, and then place them atop the appropriate pile of objects.

Step by step, we were moving toward more abstract work, but always using the concrete thing being represented by the printed word as part of our learning. The following lesson, he was given clearly printed labels for each item. Again, he laid out the two blends, sorted the objects, but now he would also try to figure out which word labeled each object. It was a project we did together, of course, but the beauty was that he was absolutely grasping why each scribble on a slip of paper represented a very real thing, because the presence of the physical object was always part of his learning. The next day, he sorted labels before adding the matching objects. Only once this process had been totally mastered, did he execute the entire blend sorting with text alone. And once that had all happened, we again went to the "object jar" for him to select the familiar items…and this time, he would be making the labels (that's spelling!). Using wooden letters, he built the blends and eventually the words for each, proving beyond a doubt that through the use of three-dimensional objects (never two-dimensional representational pictures), he now so completely "owned" the concept that he could read and build the "language labels" and know *why* they were, not just that they were.

Further examples could be endless. Grammar, my old love, is absolutely essential for clarity of speech and writing. And what is more human than wanting to be understood? But when I taught in the schools, I remember being explicitly told not to bother teaching grammar – it wasn't on "the test." I was confounded. My middle schoolers routinely turned in work wrought with run-ons and fragments, leaving readers confused and their expressive efforts frustrated. How does one understand that an idea has been incompletely communicated without knowing the basic concepts of word functions?

The materials I used in my home classroom involve three-dimensional wooden representations of the different parts of speech, explored to varying levels of complexity depending upon the age and readiness of the child. The shapes engage sensorial absorption of the work done by particular types of words. For example, the child first encounters a solid black pyramid (and yes, herein also is a concrete connection with geometry). It is large, heavy, solid, and stationary. My children have felt its weight and can see its immobility. So when contrasted soon afterwards with the kinetic energy of the rolling, red wooden ball, it is easy to guess which kind of word is dynamic and which is static. "Nomen," the Latin word for name, is the basis for our word "noun." If I ask you to go get me the globe, you could. If I ask you to go touch the doorframe, you could. I could even ask you to go to the porch. But if I ask you to please find the…and never continue, you would have no idea what I wanted. I have not named any thing, or person, or even place; I have not used a noun, a named item. In writing, that usually means you have an incomplete sentence, and that I cannot understand what you think you have made clear (a big problem for us mindblind Aspies). Static, and very obviously important, the weight and stability of the solid black pyramid tell the child the work of a noun better than any definition ever could.

That dynamic red ball, you might guess, is a verb. Likened to our sun, the active, burning star fueling all life activity on Earth, verbs are the energy of our communication. And as a child rolls, tosses, spins, and catches that physical ball, he begins to internalize "verb as energy" through his own body.

The process goes further. Articles, adjectives, and pronouns are all variations on the pyramid, tangibly reminding the child of their association with "named" things, people, and ideas. Conjunctions are represented by a pink wooden bar, and are taught using a thin pink ribbon to tie together groups of flowers, so suddenly three separate blossoms are one group of red *and* pink *and* yellow all bound together in one vase.

Intricate steps come in between – sentences analyzed by allowing the child to stamp colored representations of the grammar shapes on printed sentence strips. Eventually, the child must write original sentences according to patterns of stamped shapes.

You will recall my love of grammar a million years ago. Why? Like Lego bricks, it's about small pieces fitting together, and when properly used, those pieces can create masterpieces. Obviously, I love to write. But I had to learn how and when and why to use this turn of phrase versus another. Otherwise, any thoughts I had that were worth sharing would never make it out onto a page with much power or possibility. The same is true for your Asperkids. My daughter has dysgraphia – a writing disability, common among Asperkids, that profoundly impairs handwriting, and disrupts idea organization and expressive thought flow. Yet having been able to learn through concrete means why she needs certain types of words to get her ideas across (the specific word choices being hers alone), her written work is vastly more communicative of the growing person within.

Theory of mind issues make it easy for Aspies to get stuck in our own heads, so early instruction in a "global" community or larger notion of humanity is paramount. As a conscientious adult, I think it is profoundly important that Asperkids be given conscious instruction in their place in a larger world. In fact, I wrote a book for my children called "My Address" in which they learn to see their place in creation beginning all the way from the furthest edges of the universe to their own front steps. Essentially, I took the abstract idea of "who am I and where do I fit in?" and answered it in very concrete terms – almost as if addressing a cosmic envelope.

In the functional geography lessons enjoyed even by my five-year-old, I seek to continue developing that perspective. There is a *lot* going on around us! One of my (and the kids') favorite concrete-to-abstract lessons involved rolling out slabs of clay together, and then allowing the children to copy the manner in which I sliced my clay, fitting the "positive" slab into the bottom of one small, rectangular loaf tin. The "negative" shapes cut from the slab went into another identical baking tin. We then used child-sized pitchers to pour water (dyed brightly with blue food coloring) into whatever open spaces were left around the cut slabs. They fingered the pliable clay and teasingly splashed the azure waves, then I brought out drawn illustrations of blue and brownish shapes that looked exactly like the creations they had made, and they matched cards to containers. Then they were given the same cards with labels – peninsula, gulf, island, and lake.

Having done the rolling and cutting of the "land," and pouring the waters themselves, this was no theoretical discussion. With their own (now slimy) hands, they'd made bits of the world in our kitchen. By touching, moving, experiencing, and then deducing, they proclaimed that each landform had an opposite version in the water!

Next came written definitions of each (which my daughter read aloud as her brother listened), and finally photographs of real landforms for them to categorize. When we were done, they began chattering on about our Disney cruise from the month before; they'd watched the onboard real-time map show our changing position, and remembered how the ship had gone around the Florida peninsula, and into the Gulf of Mexico. Excited, they raced off for the atlas, searching for other peninsulas, capes, lakes, and islands on the pages. The world was theirs to explore.

Homemade marbles

From mere modeling clay, these little kids were able to establish a more substantial understanding of the Earth around them than most adults have, and from there, a deeper appreciation for the wonder of creation in general. A "Clock of Eras" gives the kids a clear visual depiction of the relative amounts of time it took for Earth to form and for different types of life to develop, while a 100 foot "Long Black Strip" dramatically illustrates the expanse of time since Earth's creation, tipped at the very end by a ½-inch narrow white band – the proportionate time of human existence. As my daughter put it one day, time is hard to imagine. Space is hard to imagine. These tools make you feel small, but still very important to the whole thing working out right. Humility, I believe that's called, and more than a little bit of perspective.

Combining sensory work and learning, the illustration shows homemade marbles which we kneaded, mixed, and rolled out of polymer clay, then baked hard. The lesson included the effects of temperature on states of matter, the historical game of marbles and how kids played in the past, color-mixing, and finally, the construction of a marble run to watch centripetal force in action.

Drawing conclusions

Obviously, the specific curriculum examples I've explained are geared toward the elementary student; that is because my own Asperkids are young. However, having *been* an older Asperkid myself, I firmly believe that no matter what the age level or sophistication of the student, Aspies will greatly benefit from the process of experiencing the concrete, being given appropriate language, learning the label (which may, at some stages, be in foreign languages, musical scores, chemical compounds), then being asked to make higher-level connections. The world is interconnected; thoughts are, too. In days gone by, great thinkers like Leonardo da Vinci and Einstein regularly moved from mechanics to music to philosophical conjecture; it was not thought unusual for a painter to also be an alchemist, or a priest to be an astronomer.

So allow and encourage that learner to connect botany to psychology, or science to religion. Use technology as much as possible, and reuse more elementary concrete concepts as a way of making new information less unfamiliar. For example, the same grammar blocks once used to explain one's native language facilitate the natural understanding of second or third languages. Writing projects – even for older kids – can be made more multisensory; use visual organizers (even though the impulsive Aspie may not like the idea) and engage them in the communication process by encouraging the use of audio and visual components in presentations. Utilize ancient calendars and time-measurement systems as math practice, for cultural understanding or history work. How much more satisfying to practice geometric concepts by pretending to give directions to stone masons at the Great Pyramid of Giza than to just do protractor drills, not really knowing why anyone would bother learning this in the first place! Logic matters. A lot. For Asperkids of all ages, the reason behind the effort *has* to be explained. An Aspie mind, naturally tuned for intense, progressive thinking, is a precious thing. Accessed correctly, nurtured continuously, and encouraged repeatedly through frustration and success, these kids are capable of anything.

Though we may play and learn differently than our neurotypical counterparts, Aspies are profoundly creative and imaginative, in our own ways, in our own time. Technological prowess is as innovative as painting. And if there is a lesson to be had here, it is this: your Asperkid is not lazy, stupid, or careless. She is different. He is capable. But to be the best he or she can be, an Asperkid should learn in ways that support their need for logic, fact, sentient experiences and the tangible embodiment of abstractions. If you teach, try to adjust your approach or tools. If you parent, make sure your child is getting what he needs to support his natural learning inclinations in school and at home – because the truth is, he needs you.

Last week I ran into a former student, now all grown-up and married. Sweet Mariel had been in a class chock full of kids the schools had disregarded and disrespected. Most were leery of teachers and ready to drop out; I remember having to, at first, trick them into class debates by asking them to analyze art in literature class or discuss Bruce Springsteen lyrics as "poetry" (they are!). Complications in my pregnancy had forced me to leave after only two months – but the impact they had made on my heart was still memorable.

Now, more than a decade later, my student and I recognized one another and hugged. Then, in the middle of the office where she works, this young lady told everyone that, "This is my favorite teacher *ever*. She made us feel like we mattered when everyone said we didn't. She showed us ways we were smart. She made me believe in myself when no one else did." Wow. It doesn't get any better than that. What an honor to have been her teacher and to get to hear – years later – that the confidence, creativity, and respect of a trusted adult can change everything for young people on the edge. I was lucky then to be her teacher. But I am even luckier now to be a guide for my own amazing Asperkids, as you get to be for yours. And now that we all know better, we can all do better, too – for the sake of the kids. Let's not just tell them they are smart, or that they can do it. Nope, let's pretend our Asperkids are all from Missouri, and *show* them how amazing they can be.

4 DETOUR – THIS WAY
Getting Around Learning Challenges

My grandfather had a saying: "Before you start a road trip, make sure you have a full tank of gas and time to get there." Understated wisdom. After all, who really anticipates getting lost? You have your plans, know the way from Point A to Point B, and then off you go. Yet no matter how well prepared you are with GPS or maps, inevitably, some road sign is missing or some lane is closed. What then? You adapt. Maybe you call someone on your cell phone, or maybe you stop at a gas station. Maybe you even just drive around a while until you figure out what to do. If you have started with a full tank and plenty of time, you have no worries. You have the resources you need to keep moving and the freedom to find your way. The route may end up being a little different; you may not be the first to arrive. Eventually, though, you will get where you need to be.

Such is teaching a child with any kind of learning differences. Asperkids have the jackpot in that regard. Many Aspies, who may already battle anxiety, confidence issues, and some OCD tendencies, must also manage real roadblocks like working memory problems, dyslexia, dysgraphia, ADHD, visual or auditory processing issues, hypotonia (low muscle tone), motor planning problems, or sensory integration issues. Unlike neurotypical kids who have learning disabilities, Asperkids also inherently think, feel, and react differently than others; they are starting off with the deck already stacked against them.

Several parents have watched me work with these kids and said aloud how they marvel at my patience. That almost makes me laugh (and I'm sure my kids wouldn't always agree). I am one of the most *imp*atient people I know! It's just that I feel such great sympathy for the underdog; I always have. These children, who already have so much to figure out – so much that other people take for granted – have to face yet another battle when their bodies act against them. Once more, they give it their best, and end up feeling like they have disappointed their loved ones or that they are stupid, and simply give up.

No, I wouldn't characterize myself as patient – but as acting in a very logical if/then way. If my husband, a Type 1 (juvenile) diabetic, eats and does not take insulin, he will die. I could yell at him. I could call him names, stomp off, but none of that is going to change the fact that his pancreas doesn't work like mine. In a medical context, most anyone can see how ridiculous that kind of solution sounds. Instead (here's the "then"), he wears a mechanical pump that acts like an artificial pancreas by delivering what he needs in an alternative way.

Learning disabilities are no different than medical ones. Like my husband needs his insulin pump, kids who suffer real challenges to their learning also need their delivery systems to be altered. Like any real physical issues, learning disabilities have biological origins and will hinder daily living unless properly addressed. So my "patience" is really just the logical response to understanding a factual reality.

On top of what any kid with learning disabilities faces, Asperkids have even more to tackle. The idea of being bright but having real problems getting information in and clear responses out throws most every teacher for a loop. In our family, that kind of response broke my children's spirits. Quickly, they went from believing they were smart to calling themselves "stupid." Even they couldn't understand how they could do some things so well, and yet not be able to manage others at all. The only answer, they concluded, was that they were dumb, or bad, or "just not good at this." No one wants to feel like a failure, and it didn't take long for those children to avoid whatever made them feel badly about themselves, cutting corners, having meltdowns – you know the drill.

And I will be honest that we still struggle against resistance at times. That isn't particularly unique to Asperkids. I can't stand loading or unloading the dishwasher, so you can guess which task I avoid in the kitchen as long as possible.

But when it comes right down to it, my grandfather's commonsense advice still stands. Basically, we have to be prepared to take some serious detours when instructing our children. Already, we've talked about two of the most important elements of differentiated education for Asperkids: the artful use of special interests in multidisciplinary learning, and the repeated use of concrete materials to introduce and refresh abstract concepts. The third point is that even when making these adjustments in *what* information is directed toward the child, *how* it reaches him, and *how* mastery is demonstrated must also be changed.

Since forever, my daughter would state a problem – like, "My fork fell." Then, she would look at me blankly. Did she not feel like getting up for a replacement? Maybe. Certainly I like it when folks do something for me. But that really didn't seem to be the problem. It almost seemed as if she didn't know what to do about even such a simple predicament. Years later, her littler brother started doing the same thing. "I'm thirsty," he would say. Then, nothing. A spectrum-mommy friend of mine noticed this at my house, and mentioned that her son did the same sort of thing. Keenly observant, she guessed that it was a theory of mind sort of trouble. Unable to step outside their own shoes, they literally couldn't figure out what someone else could do in order to remedy the problem.

Interesting theory, I had to admit. So, I gave it a whirl, and the next time my son observed a problem without solving it or speculating on how to solve it, I made him break down the steps. Using the good ol' if/then, I began a dialogue. If you are thirsty, then what do you need? A drink. OK, if you want a drink, then what do you need? A cup and my juice. If you want those things, then where should you go? To the cabinet for the cup and to the fridge for my juice pitcher. "Oh! OK!" Up he jumped. We still had to walk through retrieving the glass, then the pitcher, then pouring the juice, then putting the pitcher away and closing the door, then carefully bringing the filled glass to the table – but we had gotten the ball rolling.

For certain, figuring out ways to solve seemingly obvious problems is an ongoing challenge for Asperkids. Not wanting to break the rules by coming out of his room naked, my five-year-old found himself in a predicament the other night. While changing into pajamas, he found that he couldn't open the package of pull-ups needed for overnight use. Feeling stuck and utterly caught between the directives to follow his bedtime routine and not come out of the room unclothed, he started screaming. "Help! Help!" I heard, echoing urgently down the hallway. Once I got there and figured out the problem, we talked out some possible solutions he might have tried. Eventually, he realized that he could've put on a robe or underwear to go find assistance. But without guidance, he couldn't have gotten to that point. Although I know these are the moments when teachers and caregivers throw up their hands in disbelief, no amount of yelling or short temper would have given this Asperkid the cognitive guidance he needed.

It is that way for most of these children, no matter how "smart." Last winter, our then seven-year-old daughter went outside without a jacket or shoes to retrieve something from the car. Not realizing she'd darted out, I locked the front door. About 15 minutes later, I was frantic, searching high and low. And then I noticed, through the transom glass, a little girl huddled on the front porch, right next to the door. I ran to let her in; she told me what had happened and that she couldn't get back inside. To be honest, this mommy was heartbroken. Never had it occurred to my brilliant little girl to ring the doorbell, or go to the garage or back door – both of which were unlocked. Instead, she sat alone in the frigid winter air, lost on her own front steps.

In the classroom, the presentation of such problem-solving troubles is actually pretty similar. However, it's usually mistaken for apathy, laziness, or lack of understanding of curricular material. Recently, my daughter was diagnosed by a clinical psychologist with expressive language disorder (written and spoken) which may yet turn out to be part of dyslexia; yet not long ago, she was told not to be "lazy" by a special education teacher who corrected her handwriting. But as the psychologist noted in her report, "it is quite possible that she is so bright that her disabilities have largely been masked." Having become my daughter's teacher by happenstance, I wasn't satisfied with poor execution that didn't match the desire to perform. The emotional breakdowns, anger, and depression I saw at home told me something was really amiss. So, I hyperfocused on the data before me, looking at her skills with a fine-tooth comb. The evidence was clear to me within just a few months of teaching; there was a real learning disorder going on here that was being overlooked by a lot of professionals who just saw a smart kid not owning her potential.

Instead of just "messy" writing, I spied odd reversals and transpositions in her writing. They were inconsistent, yes, and not as frequent as in a "typical" dyslexic's, but her psychologist agreed they were "of concern" in a child with such cognitive capability. I recorded wild swings in scores – between 62 percent on written and 100 percent on oral examinations of the exact same questions. Visual memory challenges left her in tears. And in the end, we now know "officially" that my daughter (and my son, and lots of Aspies like them!) has actual learning disabilities that conventional observation dismissed because of her overall intelligence. Yet by definition, people diagnosed with Asperger syndrome have an IQ that is, at the least, within the "normal" range. With most of the kids I've met, it seems that far above average is more common.

Dr. Asperger himself is widely known to have opined that for success in some fields, "a dash of autism is essential." The problem for our kids is that, often, they are "too bright" to receive educational or therapeutic support, even if they have legitimate deficits in learning. If Aspies' "low scores" aren't low "enough" (though huge discrepancies exist between skill sets which should be closely aligned), then kids may not be guaranteed any academic or therapeutic services. Clearly, though, the emotional strife caused by understanding something but not being able to express it logically or being able to read better than most but still reversing letters or transposing numbers isn't placated by being told, "You're not bad enough off to qualify." Not for lack of care, but more for lack of funding and understanding of Asperger's, the "system" essentially has to wait for our kids to fail (and thus, feel like a failure) before stepping in. I've always found that ironic, as the mantra we hear over and over for classically autistic children is that early intervention is the key to unlocking success. Isn't that also true for our Asperkids, who also fall on the spectrum?

For example, my five-year-old son knows all his phonemes, and can use letter blend cards to spell relatively complicated words like "check" or "rain." Yet the other day, we were having a sound scavenger hunt around the house and he drew the "oy" card, which he has known definitively for months. Yet suddenly, he couldn't even identify the letter "y." He absolutely had no idea what that letter was called – which he has known since toddlerhood. How to feel self-defeated in a microsecond. On both an emotional level and academic level, it's easy to see why he got so upset and so wants to avoid reading now. Desperate to help, I switched the game and just asked him to grab the label for the "shell" from the pile on the floor – and he did, with no trouble at all. His (wonderful) preschool teachers don't suspect a thing; they don't know what he can do (he won't show them and risk failing), so they just think he can't read yet. He scores far above average on intelligence testing and now tells them that he is going out on Halloween not just as a mummy, but as the mummy of Pharaoh Ramses II. This is not a child that is sending up red flags anywhere – except when his parents insisted that special eyes take a closer look. Then, and only then, the psychologist and reading specialists clearly recognized the warning signs.

I would argue that *all* Asperkids be monitored closely for learning disorders by professionals who will not be blinded by intelligence but be sensitive to inconsistencies. At present, that responsibility lies largely, and unfairly, with families, something I desperately hope will change. Just a few years ago, I was very clearly told by one exceptional children's administrator that her job wasn't to ensure that any student reached their "full potential," just that they passed the grade. As a mother *and* as a teacher, that simply is not alright with me.

Even when they are having a hard time in classes, it can be difficult to tell, I know. Asperkids often choose not to ask for help from their teachers. Sometimes, like neurotypical peers, they just don't want to look "dumb." More frequently, they know they aren't "getting" something, but they aren't sure what it is that they don't "get." If that's the case, how do you ask for help? Certainly, even as an adult, I have been part of group conversations where I have obviously missed something important, spending too much thought on an unimportant detail. Not wanting to appear rude or self-absorbed – and not even very clear as to what I have missed or when I lost track of things – I usually just bluff my way along.

Kids are the same way. These children cannot tell you what they don't know. They cannot say to you, "My mindblindness and problem-solving issues are getting in my way right now, so all I can perceive is the feeling of frustration or thirst or exhaustion or overload rather than actually being able to process the situation and act on it." But that's what their avoidance, resistance, temper tantrums, meltdowns, and tears are telling you. As the grown-up, it is up to you to translate behavior (however egregious) into the emotion behind it (fear of failure, confusion, anxiety) and react to that emotion, rather than the behavior (not always easy, I *know*, trust me).

Angry outbursts are like bandages to wounds – the anger isn't really what you're facing. Though it can emerge from 0 to 60 in five seconds flat, anger is the human attempt to protect feelings of sadness, humiliation, rejection, or fear. Address only the anger, and you have solved nothing save to make yourself feel better in the short term. The dynamics haven't changed because the underlying issue hasn't changed. To be clear, I am not suggesting poor behavior be ignored. On the contrary, fair and immediate response to hurtful actions or words is not only appropriate – it's necessary. (If kids behave badly at our house, they must walk up and down the stairs for prescribed periods of time – whining or complaining only earns extra minutes.) But poor behavior can be discussed much more effectively in times of calm.

Within the context of Asperger's, it is supremely important that caregivers tease out feelings from actions; they often are very different. And in order for you to truly change the child's resistant behavior – whether in learning academic, social or life skills – you have to get to the root of the discontent.

Case in point: Aspies are supposed to love visual aids, charts, and so on, and indeed, my daughter got very frustrated when her teachers failed to post a day's schedule. So, when she not only failed to follow the visual "morning/evening" routine chart in her bedroom, but also adamantly refused to use it (complete with shouting matches), I realized the solution was not fitting the underlying problem. If she was this angry, she was probably actually feeling sad, embarrassed, or afraid. Of what, though, I wasn't entirely certain.

Although I had my suspicions, I waited until things were calmed down for both of us. Then, I asked her which of those feelings matched hers; sure enough, she tearfully admitted that the reason she "hated" the chart and every other "helpful reminder" type of list pasted on her desks, in her binders, on her folders, and on the wall was that they made her feel stupid and embarrassed at needing extra help. And there it was. All we had to do was to get around the issue of wounded pride, and we'd be OK. So, I showed her my own check-off lists (and how I often add "just-completed" tasks so I can cross them out right away), and we figured out a way that her daily routine chart (which we both were able to agree was, at least for now, needed) would be a reminder of something positive rather than of something negative (her disorganization, ADHD, etc.). Enter the special interest "Athena" version of the charts as shared in Chapter 2, and suddenly looking at those charts made her smile rather than wince. We gave it a progressive timeline, establishing clear steps for weaning her off the chart over a few months' time, if she wanted that. By setting up a finite ending and a palatable appeal, the underlying emotion had been respected, the behavior changed, and the desired result – a tidier room – is a reality.

Similarly, with scholastics, what we must do for our Asperkids is to discern what precisely is making our children resist a learning task, and what *feeling* precipitates their defiant, evasive, or self-deprecating behaviors. Only then can we help a student devise her own step-by-step solutions, or creatively provide a detour around the learning disability.

The first step is to give that child a "full tank of fuel." That is, provide the Asperkid with multiple problem-solving methods for any subject. Couched in the fact that Athena, my Aspergirl's special interest favorite, is the Greek goddess of strategy, I have overtly explained to her that she will like some tactics over others (alter that to Jedi training, paleontological dig methodologies – whatever appeals most to your child). Only after I am sure she has a whole bunch of ways to tackle most any type of assignment does she earn the chance to choose her approach. However, each week brings at least one "review" of a method that has gone unused for a while, simply to ensure that her arsenal remains full and ready.

For example, in the effort to help her remember multiplication facts, I have employed visual, auditory, and kinetic learning strategies. We have "School House Rocks" DVDs, iPad apps, at least ten different Montessori tools, and silly stories that associate equations with funny pictures. Some are definite favorites, others less so. But the point is that she will always have a mental toolbox from which to pull an approach when she is asked to solve a problem on her own. Success isn't a correct answer; it's the self-confidence that your Asperkid is a capable person.

"You are a prosthetic frontal lobe!" Now I've been called a lot of things before, but there's a first. When my children's psychologist said this, beaming at me, I figured it must be a good thing, though. And it is. But, how about a little bit of background. Within the first month of homeschooling, I noticed that, although my Aspergirl's reading fluency was literally in the 99.9th percentile, her response to open-ended comprehension questions was often wrong – close – but not exactly right. Even if she was answering verbally, she was making a lot of mistakes. Generally, her teachers had blamed this on her being too lazy or not caring enough to take the time to answer correctly. But I know my child and even when she plays otherwise (maybe then the most), she cares powerfully about getting things right. There had to be more to the story. So, I did what I always do – I sat back and watched for patterns.

And there they were. It seemed that the issue wasn't so much that she hadn't understood the story, but that her precise memory of the facts was off, thus leading her to make errors in responding to critical thinking challenges. Each time I would ask her a question about the chapter we'd read aloud together, she would try to instantly reply, get it wrong, and then argue as to why she was actually right. My showing her proof of the mistake, no matter how gently, only fanned the flames of insecurity – which blew up into a giant, bombastic mess. Clearly, I needed to get her to stop and think before making the mistake to begin with.

The topic we happened to be studying was a novel about Native Americans. Going with the "theme" and zero planning, I imagined the old tomahawk beat from my high school football games, took her hand in mine, and started thumping a rhythm on her leg. BUM-bum-bum-bum. BUM-bum-bum-bum. Over and over I chanted and thumped. She felt me, she heard me – there was nothing to defend against. It was just a steady rhythm. And then I added words.

"STOP"-bum-bum-bum. "LOOK"-bum-bum-bum. "THINK"-bum-bum-bum. "ACT"-bum-bum-bum. The chant repeated, and I finally got her to say it along with me. Then, we tried anew. I asked her a question about the story – but before she could reply, I cut her off, thumping her leg and chanting STOP, LOOK, THINK, ACT. Before she was allowed to answer me, she had to close her mouth. That was the STOP. No impulsive responses. Then, she had to LOOK for the relevant facts within the text (I helped her as needed). In actively revisiting the source, she had to reengage with the information she thought she knew, versus what was actually there. Perception versus fact, in black and white. Best of all, when she could be the first to "discover" the correct facts upon which she'd have to draw conclusions, she "saved face." How much better to teach an Asperkid the best way to manage a problem before taking it on, than to have to focus my attention (and hers) on correcting mistakes after the fact?

Using the now-verified, accurate facts, this Aspergirl had to THINK to solve the problem. And more often than not, she was absolutely able to make the required higher-level deductions and/or associations. Then, she could finally ACT. In this case, it meant she could answer. Almost every time (with guidance and discussion as needed), she got it right.

My littler Asperkid also uses this method for completely non-academic problem-solving tasks, like taking the recycling out to the garage. Inevitably, he would pick up the bin and walk to the garage door, which was still shut, and call for someone to help him open it. By getting him to understand the STOP, LOOK, THINK, ACT method (I can sometimes hear him chanting under his breath!), either he will open the door first or put the bin down, open the door, and then walk out. He has solved the problem independently because he has stopped, surveyed the situation, thought about it more carefully, and then moved forward.

So when my children's psychologist called me a prosthetic frontal lobe, what did she mean? As in the anecdotes throughout this chapter, we Aspies often have areas of deficit when it comes to executive function, which largely involves planning and strategizing. We are impulsive, and perhaps don't stop long enough to check ourselves or verify that our emotions, responses, or behaviors match the reality of a situation. The brain's frontal lobe, I have since learned, includes response inhibition and impulse control. So that's what our chant and patting "STOP, LOOK, THINK, ACT" did when their minds couldn't. To us, it was an obvious solution, organically created without planning and lovingly passed from one generation of Aspie to the next.

At home, at school, and out in the bigger world, we can help get our Asperkids where they need to be, even if the route is different or it takes a little longer. How? Well, now that their gas tanks are full, let's take a look at a couple of available detours.

A "prepared environment": setting the stage

Almost every Aspie has attention problems. It seems to be a given of our make-up, and it makes staying organized pretty darned tough. Some of us become label-maker addicts (guilty), others just leave a perpetual stream of stuff in their wake without ever noticing (my hubby).

Books ad nauseam have been written about tackling ADHD and sensory integration problems, and many of them are good – everyone has a method that works best for them, be it medicine, brushing therapy, digital calendars that sync family schedules, or good old-fashioned to-do lists. That issue is super-important, but well addressed elsewhere.

On the other hand, there is one issue which I think deserves special note in minimizing the distractions in Asperkids' worlds. The philosophy is a Montessori phrase called "preparing the environment." Dr. Maria Montessori's first students were impoverished street children, whom she set out to prove were as "teachable" as any others. Later, she would attest that a significant element of her success with these forgotten children came from the careful preparation of a uncluttered, "child-centered," predictable environment. And as anyone who loves an Asperkid knows, predictability is of heightened import for our children because it relieves anxiety and minimizes perseveration (getting stuck on one, often nonessential, thought or worry).

Dr. Montessori observed that these first students, much like our often-worried, routine-bound Asperkids, felt safer and more self-sufficient because of the carefully laid out order around them. Nothing was off-limits; each item was usable, child-sized, aesthetically pleasing, and accessible. Whether floor mat, wooden container, vinyl mat, heavy metal platter, or real glass pitcher, everything had a purpose and a place. She called this layout the "prepared environment," and believed that it had a powerful influence on the way a developing mind learns. Now imagine the potency of that approach with regard to our easily distracted, easily frustrated, often reluctant learners!

The way in which a learning environment is laid out is extremely significant to the way that Asperkids can focus on, absorb, and retain information. We teachers are notorious for "brightening" our classrooms. Who wants to look at painted cinderblocks, after all? So we go a little bit crazy at the teacher supply stores. You know exactly what I mean – posters with funny animal faces and inspiring sayings. Alphabet chains, world maps, birthday charts, student work, borders, displays in every corner – with every good intention, we try to fashion a happy place where students will want to spend their time. After touring one kindergarten classroom, my husband commented that it felt "like a carnival in there." It wasn't a compliment.

For Aspies, and arguably for developing minds in general, less is definitely more. Visual noise pollution is just as deafening to the intake of information as is auditory distraction. Pull down the posters or, at the very least, put them in the rear of the room. Deaden the scratching of chair feet by slipping them into cut-open tennis balls. Dull the general schoolroom echo with neutrally colored area rugs. In my own classroom, I guess I was letting my sensory sensitivity drive design – and students ended up thanking me for it. The clean lines of black and white photographic architectural posters were the choice for visuals, and only behind or far off to the side. We almost never lit the awful fluorescent overhead light, relying on the natural ambient light. And I hung earth-toned curtains by the windows to soften the room's harsh "institutional" acoustics. The corner featured a cushiony couch (my grandmother's discard) for student use, a floor lamp with a soft reading bulb, and a CD player churning out the London Symphony Orchestra. Universally, the kids (of all ages) loved it. In other words, for her students and for mine, Dr. Montessori's layout was right on target.

It is also true for an Asperkid's home. In the last year, I have literally overhauled our entire playroom and family room, modeling them after the "prepared environment" plan. Lots of toys and furniture were donated to Goodwill – they didn't do anything, really, but clutter. The goal was that everything was in reach, child sized, and there for a reason. Trust me, I know that what I'm asking you to recreate isn't simple. But then, everything about Asperger's requires a bit more planning and energy. I didn't redo the rooms on a big budget, just with a lot of thought. Open shelves and cubbies came from Target or Ikea, wooden trays, baskets, and small containers were from Wal-Mart and Hobby Lobby. In the end, it looks beautiful.

But more important than how it looks, I can't overstate the change the surroundings have made in the way the kids learn and behave. They are so much more self-sufficient, and proud of themselves for it. They don't have to spend a lot of time trying to remember where a particular book, manipulative, or art supply is. Everything is predictable, part of learning (or purposeful play), and easily picked up. Their focus is better, their confidence improved and, to quote them, even though lots of toys disappeared (Mom did that undercover – otherwise we would've had panic attacks), "it's a lot more playable in here!" So before you do anything else, make sure the places you ask Asperkids to inhabit are calming, uncluttered, sized appropriately and positive. It is worth the investment. By preparing their learning environment in this way, you are helping to improve their (and their neurotypical peers') concentration, step-by-step processing, and independent achievement.

The eyes (and ears) have it: reading, retention, and refusal

OK, before I begin here, I have to give a shout-out to all the parents and teachers who equate reading skills with intelligence. Hear ya! That was me! First – newsflash. They are *not* one and the same. My daughter read chapter books by age three and now, at age eight, reads (and comprehends) on a college level. She was skipped a grade upon entering a private school (with disastrous consequences) largely because of her reading. Here's the kicker – I am also pretty sure she is dyslexic. She flips letters and reads words that aren't there. Her little brother has an IQ in the "very superior" range (as high as it gets), yet his focus and problems with symbol imagery led him to write "no" when asked to write "on" (Freud would have a field day, I know), and score only at an "average" for his age in reading skills, though I know (and testing shows) for certain that he can do far more.

I tell you all of this because as a parent and teacher, I do not want any other caring adult to dismiss the possibility of legitimate symbol-based learning disorders among even the most proficient readers or young children whose aptitude says they should be doing more than they are. Don't wait it out. Step in and see. No one snaps out of problematic neurological hardwiring, but all children (no matter the IQ) are very aware of when they are not able to perform as they sense they should.

So whether or not your Asperkid has a formal diagnosis of dyslexia, attention deficit disorder (ADD) or ADHD (something pretty much *every* Asperkid has), the concerns are the same: disconnect between text and comprehension, information/skill retention, and inability to stay on task. As we all know, if you can't read directions clearly, you are not going to know what to do, how to answer, or be able to benefit from the imagination or information being presented. It doesn't matter if you are a math whiz or history natural, if you can't get what you need from the writing in front of you (whether they are numbers or letters), or you forget it by the time the next lesson comes up, you're stuck. The answer, it seems, lies in yet another detour. When one road is out, find another way in.

Solutions
BELLS, E-READERS, AND MAGNIFIERS

No free advertising dollars earned here, I promise, but I am a big fan of the sensory-cognitive learning processes utilized at Lindamood-Bell Learning Processes Centers internationally (see Resources). Essentially, their program breaks the reading process into specific visualizing processes which enhance concept and symbol imagery. In English, that means that they help concrete-minded thinkers like Asperkids more readily bind audible phonemes or physical objects to abstract symbols (letters, numbers, words, and equations). My daughter can do complex geometry but can't remember that $6 \times 7 = 42$, because in her head "6" still doesn't concretely enough represent that quantity. Same goes for why she wants to write a "g" and ends up making an "m" or can't succinctly summarize her thoughts (expressive disorder). Talk about frustrating! So, if Lindamood-Bell learning support is an option for your child, even if you think the issue isn't true dyslexia, explore it. If you're a teacher, investigate the many opportunities they have for continuing education training for educators. It really is worth it.

Sometimes the best thing you can do for a reluctant reader is to work on the packaging. Last fall, I got a fabulous birthday present: an e-reader. Oh, sure, it was fun, instant, and portable, and all the things that the maker advertised. Little did I know, there would be another benefit to this birthday gift. Drawn to the newest techno-gadget in the house, my Aspergirl immediately asked to explore it. And, together, we even downloaded a book for her. But when she started to read, she quickly handed it back. "It's too small," she shrugged. Wait – suddenly, we had an option that we hadn't before. I could increase the font size dramatically, thereby also providing ample "white space" around the words to help her eyes focus where they should and rest where they shouldn't. So, with hope, I showed her how to bump up the text size to "Extra Extra Large," and voilà! It was perfect!

Now that e-reader apps are available for free on almost every operating system for smartphones (e.g. Blackberry, iPhone) and tablets (e.g. iPad, Android), they really should be made accessible to any child who needs them. Almost any book is now available electronically, and the whole concept appeals to the technologically adept Asperkid. Enlarging the font as he or she wants, your Asperkid can then reclaim some of the joy of reading that "dancing letters" or "tired eyes" have stolen. And for younger kids, many discount retail stores stock endless handheld devices or read-aloud "pens" that are just as attractive. Tech it up and every Asperkid will be more interested.

You can also try an "old-school" approach. Page-sized magnifiers, often used by older people or those who are visually impaired, will enlarge the text and do, indeed, offer some improvement. But at least from personal observation, these magnifiers are more helpful with regard to worksheets or single-paged texts. The motor control it takes to maneuver the magnification sheet and hold or turn the pages of a reading book is often more than the Asperkid can manage without frustration ending the whole endeavor. So, if that doesn't work, one more idea: my daughter actually found old-fashioned "reader" glasses pretty darned effective, too.

The point of being literate is to be able to absorb fact, enjoy fiction, and generally be inspired to do our own thinking, be it logical or fantastical. And while I personally am a die-hard bibliophile, a child with legitimate reading challenges is not going to be. Whenever the possibility allows, consider avoiding reading altogether. The choice is either to stifle their absorption of information and imagination by forcing the issue, or taking another detour. Vision is but one sense: get in to that Asperkid using some of the others!

LITERACY THROUGH LISTENING

Let's try their ears. Everyone loves to be read to. Many Asperkids still prefer to sit with a parent and listen to a story, even if they can read it quite proficiently themselves. Certainly mine do (they even make me read in British, French, or Spanish accents as they story dictates). Why? First, it is a way to connect with another person without having to invent dialogue. The story is the conversation. Time together, though scripted, is the important thing.

Frequently, reading aloud to the child drastically improves comprehension as well. Even my daughter, who has some auditory processing issues to boot, prefers Mom to read to her above all.

More than just communicating information, we are making memories and allowing Mom to explain and expand upon passing references; I know about "Percy Jackson" or "Harry Potter" or even the differences between allosaurus and tyrannosaurus because I have taken the time to experience the stories with them. As a result, we have "shorthand" that emotionally bonds us, and the kids are continuously exposed to new stories, ideas, and questions.

While not as interpersonal, audio books are wonderlands of mood and drama. They are, really, twenty-first century versions of the radio theater that captivated the entire world a hundred years ago. In minutes, complete texts can be downloaded onto an iPod or MP3, playing over headphones, throughout a room from a stereo dock, or over a car radio. Let your Asperkid build Lego or paint models while listening – rather than being a distraction, sometimes these beloved tasks increase endurance, and actually improve attention to the story. Much like a book-lover adores the feeling of being lost in his own world while turning pages, your Asperkid can be drawn in to faraway lands and long-ago times (sometimes aided in comprehension by accompanying music or sound-effects), without ever having to battle the page. This not only goes for pleasure reading, but also is a particularly potent way of supplementing classwork. If a teacher assigns a specific novel, there is absolutely no reason why your Asperkid can't engage with that very story by listening to it instead of (or at least in addition to) reading it. Often, the author is the one lending his or her voice, so who better to deliver the words, after all?

GETTING IN ANY WAY YOU CAN

Beyond specifics to one learning disability or another, I cannot emphasize enough the importance of getting your child moving and doing. If the point of learning is to educate a child about the world and then give him, as Euripides said, a "place to stand so that [he can] move it," grown-ups have to stop worrying about the rote basics (they *will* come) and get to the point: establishing a lifelong sense of curiosity, passion, and relevance.

In the 1980s, Dr. Howard Gardner published the now-famous idea that schools placed far too much emphasis on linguistic and mathematical intelligence, while ignoring children's natural inclinations toward kinesthetic (movement), musical, spatial, and other areas of proficiency (Gardner 1993). This is my ultimate plea for detour-taking, and my ultimate praise of interdisciplinary learning. One of the hardest things for Asperkids to do is to turn their attention away from their passion and to step out of their shoes into the reality of someone else. Teachers and parents have to get creative. The kids deserve it.

So, for example, if a class is learning about Native Americans, it is imperative that the adult draw from some of those other "intelligences" to pique the Asperkid's interest, draw him into the experience of the protagonist, and give a logical frame of reference to the story.

In my classroom, we did just that. We chose, recreated, and rated recipes. Watched video clips of the Calgary opening ceremonies and of artfully animated Native American creation stories, learned different methods of counting and chronicling time, and drew maps of tribal territories (imperfect, but fun!). We tried to learn and perform a native dance piece – and then went to a powwow to watch the real thing. We used wall-sized Venn diagrams to compare regions and their peoples. We wove a rug out of T-shirt strips on a hula hoop. My Asperkid went on a WebQuest (an online information scavenger hunt). We crafted native toys and played some long-forgotten games. We listened to a YouTube Cherokee language lesson. We read as many first-person novels and biographies of young Native Americans as possible. We watched *The Indian in the Cupboard* (1995). They learned to play lacrosse (sort of). We planted a garden of "the three sisters," corn, beans, and squash. And my daughter and her dad built a Lego totem. Finally, we used scrapbooking tools from the craftstore – paper punches, stencils, and stickers – to record our adventures in fun, creative ways.

Aspies need to see the logic of what they are learning: in other words, why should I bother? For one project, I got chalk, protractors, and technology involved as we put real-world application to the geometry and Earth science we'd been covering. After the project, I guided my daughter as she worked hard to summarize what she had done, seen, and deduced.

Angles in the Sky

by Maura O'Toole

The angle of the sun is a big part of the changing temperature. We checked on Star Walk[1] and learned that today, the sun's highest point above the horizon would be at 40 degrees.

My mom asked me to show what that would look like, so I used a protractor and chalk to measure and illustrate. The picture I drew is called "November 2nd at Noon."

Next, we researched and found that on the summer solstice, June 21st, the angle of the sun in our town is 78 degrees above the horizon. This creates the most hours of daylight and much warmer temperatures. We measured and drew this scene, too.

The third measurement was for December 21st, the winter solstice. It is 30 degrees, which is pretty close to today's height. The lower point in the sky means fewer hours of daylight and colder temperatures.

I observed that in summer and spring, the higher angle of the sun means there is a longer distance of sky to cover, more hours of daylight, and a warmer atmosphere. Lower angles in the fall and winter lead to fewer hours of sunlight and colder temperatures.

Angles in the sky

---

1   Star Walk is an interactive astronomy guide designed by Vito Technology, Inc. (www.vitotechnology.com).

There are a million ways to learn, to absorb, and to respond to new information. For an Asperkid to want to bother, to put forth the effort when he thinks he is stupid or is just too tired of trying and failing, it is up to the loving parent or compassionate teacher to show him that he is as he should be, and the world is his to explore.

Solution summary: reading detours

- Lindamood-Bell centers
- E-readers
- Audio books
- Being read to by parents or siblings
- Multisensory engagement with materials.

Putting pen to paper, or not: how to get around writing issues

Getting information into an Asperkid is one issue. Getting it out is a whole other challenge. Most people have never heard of dysgraphia, and until the last few years, neither had I. However, I had been seeing its effects for quite some time. From the earliest of preschool art projects, my kids have been the ones with the least proficiency. A scribble here, a line or two there. Maybe it was inattention? I wasn't sure, but I had to admit that I was surprised; for such smart kids, why didn't they seem to be able to draw or craft like their peers?

I saw the same problem as they left one coloring book after another to gather dust. Other moms would be baffled at my son's or daughter's distaste – didn't all kids like to color? I had thought so, too, but apparently not. At one birthday party, I remember overhearing another little girl look at my daughter's coloring page and wrinkle her nose. "That's bad," she said, and my little one's face fell. She had been trying her best. Needless to say, it didn't really come as a big surprise when her preschool teacher alerted me that something might be going on with her writing, or her eyes, or both.

That was four years ago. Along the way, my daughter (and then my son, to follow) has worked on fine motor issues, hand strengthening, visual perception problems, convergence problems, eye-teaming trouble, occupational therapy, vision therapy, you name it and we've done it. I have my own sets of Handwriting Without Tears building blocks to physically construct letters (see Resources), chalkboards to practice on while saying aloud the name of strokes ("big line, little curve"), a music CD to sing "Where Do You Start Your Letters? At the Top!" (Olsen 2008), and student books in which my children can write. Orton-Gillingham (see Resources) is much the same: super multisensory programs that aren't overly repetitive and incorporate visual, auditory, and kinesthetic learning styles. We have handwriting apps on the iPad and paper with raised lines so the kids can see *and* feel where the pencil should stop. But in truth, at eight years of age, unless she takes an extremely long time on each letter, my daughter's handwriting is still often illegible. Her brother's is better, but not much.

At a certain point, the message received by a child with learning difficulties changes from "This [fill in the tool or therapy or method] can help me do things better!" to "Why am I still having trouble after so much hard work?" Then the cycle of self-doubt and insecurity begins anew. Different once again feels defective, and the effort to remediate feels fruitless. As parents, we have to step in when/if we just don't see change happening to say "enough is enough" before the child crumbles. For Aspies, writing is one of those areas – and it affects almost every area of learning.

Dysgraphia, I learned from listening to Tony Attwood speak, is essentially a neurologically based condition that plagues many Aspies. It literally means "bad writing," and is the experience of having to think, while writing, of how to mechanically make the letters or numbers, no matter how many times it has been done before. That was it. I had seen my "genius-IQ" daughter flustered, angry, and snapping at a request to write something because, as she finally shouted through tears, "I can't remember how to make an 'M'!" On the writing section of a recent achievement test, the psychologist kindly noted, "If only she would have been willing to write a bit more, she would have scored much higher." The fact is, though, that no matter how much my Aspergirl has to say on a topic, she won't write it out – it's just too hard. And truly, how can we expect someone who has to actively think about the actual process of writing to also spell, punctuate, and express her ideas clearly (let alone creatively)?

For Asperkids like mine, cognitive processes are often not commensurate with motor planning, strength, or visual perception. Thus, these children face real boundaries that get in the way of expressing what they know, or of ever feeling proud of their work. Therefore, as I see it, binding the introduction of new material and/or proof of mastery to lagging writing skills unnecessarily stifles curiosity and dampens self-esteem. There are alternative routes to success.

Gavin on iPad

Using technology to develop out-of-synch skill sets. At 19 months, Gavin never would have had the dexterity to assemble tangrams, but his visual-spatial skills were flourishing. Given the aid of an iPad, he could put together complex puzzles without being limited by still-developing motor skills. The photo shows Gavin at two years using an iPad to do a map puzzle of the continents.

Sean with blue triangles

Sean's dysgraphia is so severe that he can't draw a triangle. But, using some "constructive triangles," he was able to construct a 360-degree star out of twelve 30-degree angles, and experiment with the ways in which triangles can create all other polygons – all without picking up a pencil. And just check out that proud face!

Solutions
KEYBOARDING

Tony Attwood's speech essentially gave me emotional "permission" to abandon the stringent handwriting efforts and get my little girl keyboarding. Like so many Aspies, she adores technology of any kind. So once we found the BBC's free, fabulous Dance Mat Typing program online (see Resources), everything changed. She worked on it daily, and soon was more proficient than most adults.

Every day from then on, I would provide her with a document to copy – the original was at the top of the screen; she was to type beneath (the Asperkid should never have to copy from another surface, which would require that he look down at a paper, refocus, look back at the screen, refocus, and then try to remember what to type). And there was a bonus! In her daily keyboarding practice, we had come upon a way to get my Aspergirl to also read about any subject much more willingly: sure, the special interest was omnipresent, but everything from music lyrics to poetry to science theories made appearances. She never would have copied them by hand without hours passing and emotions boiling over; on the keyboard and screen, any task was more welcome.

Here is an example of practicing keyboarding skills, integrating her history lessons, and wrapping up with her special interest – the bonus was the personal connection at the end!

Keyboarding exercise

Animism is the belief that all things in nature have spirits.

Animism is the belief that all things in nature have spirits.

The Cherokee used baskets to sift cornmeal for bread.

The Cherokee used baskets to sift cornmeal for bread.

The Iroquois called squash, corn, and beans "the three sisters."

The Iroquois called squash, corn, and beans "the three sisters."

Lacrosse was invented by the natives in the Southeast.

Lacrosse was invented by the natives in the Southeast.

Babies wore soft moss and fluffy cattail plants instead of diapers.

Babies wore soft moss and fluffy cattail plants instead of diapers.

(And for fun...) ☺

The Parthenon in Athens was the Greek temple to Athena.

The Parthenon in Athens was the Greek temple to Athena.

Greek heroes grew up listening to the fables of Aesop.

Greek heroes grew up listening to the fables of Aesop.

Maura O'Toole is funny and smart. ☺

Maura O'Toole is funny and smart. Hehe.

I love you too Mom.

While word processing, spreadsheets, presentations, and programming don't usually appear in school until late elementary to even middle or high school, for Asperkids, it must happen earlier – as early as the child can use a device. And that can be very, very young. Heck, our 18-month-old was giddily completing puzzles of continents and states because a touch screen enabled him to merely drag and drop. Use handheld electronic reading "toys" like Leap Frog's Leapster or Tag Reader, iPad, tablets, whatever you have. Give an Asperkid a lesson on Pages or Word, and he will much more readily alphabetize spelling lists, edit for punctuation, learn about percentages while coloring in pie graphs or draw, identify, and label the parts of a circle using design software. Technology isn't a nicety; for Asperkids, it is a necessity.

LETTER MANIPULATIVES

Another really good way for (primarily younger) kids to work with letters but avoid the writing process is to use sandpaper letter cards, fridge magnets, or "movable type" (wooden cut-outs of each letter available in print or cursive, and in many language styles). Asking a dysgraphic child to write out, say, the classifications of vertebrates or to spell "duck" would force him to spend more energy on the process of writing than on the scientific or phonetic task at hand.

Frustration is instant. Resignation or anger takes over. Learning is stunted. But having him sort picture cards or select (sometimes from a limited number of choices) the appropriate letters to physically build the words still demands engagement with the material and frees him from the burdens of handwriting.

STAMPS

A while back, I was telling a friend of mine about how amazed I was by the progress my son was making using the Montessori math materials. Her own little guy is on the spectrum, and she told me that he couldn't move on to those activities because he couldn't write his numbers yet. Neither could my child, I insisted. She wondered: how could my Asperkid be "writing" equations as he figured them out with his manipulatives if he couldn't write? Simple – we used rubber stamps. Most craft stores carry variously sized stamps of numbers, math symbols, punctuation, letters, and shapes. As he used beads or rods or even dinosaurs to figure out all the ways to add up to ten, I had my son stamp out his discoveries. One bead put together with nine more was stamped "$9 + 1 = 10$," making sure he used different colored ink for the ones or tens columns. To save time, sometimes I would stamp out an equation to which he would respond in kind, but usually, he really liked how clear his answers were when stamping them. He kept advancing his learning *and* could report what he discovered, all without writing a single number.

Stamping is also a beautiful way for children to explore geometry, patterns, and even grammar. Rather than using anxiety-producing tests to measure mastery, my students create projects – usually "books" – showing what they know. One example, an explanation of polygons, what they looked like, and what their names meant, was accomplished entirely through stamping the shapes and typing the text. Rubbing plates allowed my younger child to "illustrate" his book on North American animals, even though he doesn't much like to draw. Crayons and paper over the plates of salmon and coyotes provided exactly what he wanted to share with his audience. Alphabet stamps allowed him to label each picture, although he did sign his work in a flourish of crayon.

LEGO

We have even used Lego instead of written work. As we concluded the aforementioned unit on Native Americans, I asked my daughter to respond to what she understood of totem poles (carved wooden posts) by creating one that illustrated her own life; she looked sick. But no worries, she wasn't being asked to draw. No, she was to make hers out of Lego and verbally explain the significance of each part. Her eyes lit up, and the creative juices flowed. What she made was fantastic, showed clear mastery of the subject, and allowed her to engage without putting pencil to paper.

When learning about Mesopotamia, what better way to practice collaboration, perspective, and planning while having a little fun with history? The assignment was to build a Lego "ziggurat" temple to a fictitious Sumerian deity, and to write a petition that a citizen might have offered there. Hands-on work appeals to Asperkids' need for kinetic learning and provides fun opportunities to creatively engage critical thinking. This project required collaboration (tough!), perspective-taking, topical understanding, and Lego fun.

Make your own ziggurat

1. Explain to your partner what a ziggurat was, and where it was used.

2. Reread "Mesopotamian Religion" together.

3. Go online to www.librarybcds.com/5thGrade/Mesopotamian GodsandGoddesses.html with your grown-up. Choose a Mesopotamian god/goddess from the list provided to be the patron deity of your fictional, ancient town.

4. Design and build a ziggurat using city blocks, Lego, and any other materials you like. Find ways to show that it is dedicated to the god/goddess you chose. You may take pictures to document the building, and include surrounding activity to complete the diorama.

5. Take a picture of the finished product!

6. Play "Say Your (Mesopotamian) Prayers!" (see below). Decide which of their gods or goddesses an ancient Mesopotamian might have asked for help based upon a particular need.

7. Then, write a petition that someone might have offered at "your" ziggurat. Use the examples from "Ask-a-God" as a guide. Type your fictitious "request" below the photo of your construction project and present it proudly.

Make your own ziggurat rubric
What will be expected:

Directions were all followed.	Say Your Prayers! worksheet completed.
Written work is neat, spelled correctly, and has complete punctuation and capitalization.	Say Your Prayers! answers are correct.
Written project has a title that is centered and in bold font.	Original "prayer" makes sense, and shows thought. It is at least five sentences long.
Photo is included. (Can be more than one to show your building process!)	Building is creative, detailed, and shows understanding of how a ziggurat worked.

Say Your (Mesopotamian) Prayers!

The ancient Mesopotamians directed their prayers and requests for help to the gods and goddesses whose special abilities addressed their problems.

Using the website provided, decide which god or goddess each of these ancient Mesopotamians might ask for help. Write his or her name and on the line.

Dear A_____,

My grain harvest is not what it should be! I have sown and tended my fields, but still, the barley does not grow as I had hoped. Please, oh goddess of grain, grant me a plentiful crop to feed my family!

Zadu the Farmer

Dear Z_____,

My son has been having such strange dreams! Every night, he sees seven camels dancing around the walls of the ziggurat just before it crumbles. I cannot imagine what it means, but he is desperate! Please send him peaceful dreams, and reveal to us any hidden messages in those dreams you have already sent.

Malla the Mother

Dear N_____,

I have long been your loyal servant. In return, can you please protect me and my crew as we travel the River on our new invention, the sailboat? Grant us calm waters, oh my goddess.

Bilboa the Boatman

Dear M_____,

You are the god of the thunder in the sky — supreme leader who looms above all others. I beg of you to spare my home, my lord, during this season of lightning, rain, and storm, so that my family may live safely to worship you forever.

Senek the Weak

Dear N_____,

My son studies hard, oh my lord. He longs to be a scribe. We have given him all the education we can afford, and now ask you, oh, god of written words, to guide his hand and mind.

Wrika the Devoted

Lego ziggurat

SORTING CARDS

Beyond the other concrete reading tools discussed previously, sorting prewritten cards enables the child to show what she knows without writing. For example, provide a card labeled "concrete nouns" and another card labeled "abstract nouns," and ask your Asperkid to place strips of paper with examples of each under the appropriate heading. This method also works with pictures – sorting labeled photographs of solids, liquids, and gases, or fish, amphibians, and mammals into the correct group. Further the lesson by asking the child to explain what characteristics designate the classification. These materials are all easily created at home and really do push the child to both interact with and display understanding of limitless concepts.

NOMENCLATURE CARDS

Nomenclature, you may remember from high school chemistry, is the naming of something; from "nomen," the Latin word for "name," as already mentioned, it is the basis of our word "noun" – the name of a thing. On the most basic level, nomenclature means simply learning how to code/decode (write/read) the label for a thing; in other words, a child understanding that the series of letters "hanger" refers to the thing in our bedroom closets. As thinking become more sophisticated, new terminology gives children access to undiscovered ideas, perspectives, and data.

Nomenclature cards are three- or four-part paper manipulatives that engage Asperkids in the acquisition and mastery of new words, but never require dreary vocabulary sentences or too-small blanks on a worksheet. The initial "control card" features an aesthetically pleasing picture of the object being named with the written word or concept being taught. For the younger child learning to read, we'll say it is a photograph of a rooster, clearly labeled "rooster" beneath; for the older child learning about ancient Egypt, for example, it might be a photograph of three figures on beautiful papyrus artwork and the label "clothing" below. The next card features only the photograph, and separate from that is a label strip with the word. Older learners may also have a brief definition card in which the word in question is included in the explicative text, printed in bold.

At the first encounter, the child lays out the control cards – up to five or six should be the maximum terms learned at a time to maintain attention for an Asperkid. Then, the child lays out the photograph card to match each control, and then the label. Advanced students also match the correct definition card. (Typically at this point, Montessori students would be asked to copy these words and/or definitions into a notebook; I saw first-hand how that squelched the process for my daughter, and fast. However, she loves the idea of an online journal, where she records one or two definitions a day as keyboard practice.)

The next time the cards are shown, the control card is used only if necessary. Otherwise, it is laid face down to the side while the child attempts to match photographs and labels on his own. When done, he uses the control cards to check his own work and make whatever corrections are necessary, thus giving him ownership of the whole process, including any problem-solving needed to fix an error. For an Asperkid learning to read or spell, he may use movable type to build the label (while looking at the control card), and finally, he assembles the word without a model, checking back after he is through and adjusting his work as needed. After mastering a set of cards, an older child might begin to construct a "Dictionary of Ancient Egypt" or other such product to demonstrate her knowledge of the new terms.

My little boy, who can't focus for long on a book and certainly couldn't write "rooster," was suddenly profoundly successful at moving around his labels and pictures – giving him names for everything from farm animals to constellations to art supplies to woodworking tools. He was actively participating in his learning in ways that his writing skills and hand strength would otherwise inhibit.

My older Asperkids have used this process to learn everything from the positions of lines to the etymology of calendar names, from the flags of nations to the parts of a leaf. My two-year-old uses them to practice colors. From the most basic of concepts to the highest levels, nomenclature cards are a phenomenal way to acquire information and then physically engage with it without ever having to write a word or draw a line. Best of all, while they are easily purchased from any of the Montessori websites listed in the Resources section as ready-to-print PDFs, once you get the hang of the process, they are easily made at home. A little research and some basic formatting, and you have what you need.

As examples, these are some of the nomenclature cards that I made in teaching my daughter the etymology of our names for the months of the year. We tied it in to her love of ancient mythology, yes, but it also became the basis for the introduction of fractions in math and discussions on astronomy. Everything started, though, with these cards made on my home computer, printed in whole and cut into parts for her to manipulate and learn.

Control cards

May	June

Definition cards

May is the fifth month of our year. Called *Maius* in Latin, it was named after the Roman goddess Maia, protector of young plants. During this time of sowing seeds and new plant growth, the people wished to ask Maia's protection over their fragile buds so that crops and food would be plentiful at harvest time.

June is named for Juno, the queen of the Roman goddesses, and is the sixth month on our calendar. In Latin, it was called *Junius*. On June 21st, the Northern Hemisphere is tilted towards the sun more than it is at any other time, giving us the Summer Solstice, the day with the most hours of sunlight of the entire year.

LENGTHIER WRITTEN WORK: ORGANIZERS,
DICTATION, AND SCRIBING

On a conceptual level, some Aspies also find it difficult to translate their thoughts into lengthier written expression, even with the support of a keyboard or touch screen. For these kids, one of the biggest problems isn't vocabulary or understanding of what it is they are describing. The issue is being able to organize thoughts and decipher what knowledge they have that you don't – in other words, mindblindness. However, if the point of a lesson is the content rather than the presentation, please allow the child to focus his energy on the ideas he puts forth, rather than on the handwriting or manufacturing of said letters or words.

There is nothing more precious to kids with expressive challenges (possibly the most talkative in class, so don't be fooled) than visual organizers – and parent or teacher scribes. Much in the same way that I if/then'ed my son into figuring out how to alleviate his thirst by getting a drink, visual organizers force students to break their ideas into smaller, connected bits. They form a template of sorts; again, give us a model to follow, and we will do much better at creating our own versions of most anything.

Aspie mindblindness makes it frustrating for us when others don't immediately understand how we've moved from one thought to another without our clearly explaining each step in between. That's a learned skill which takes time to develop. So, the parent or teacher should first expect to annoy the Asperkid. That's right, you read correctly. You're going to tick them off. But in order to force an Aspie to learn how to slow down and laboriously explain a train of thought, you are going to initially frustrate the heck out of him. Still, you will need to say things like, "What I hear you saying is…" and reflect back the actual image or idea the Asperkid is conveying. In all likelihood, it's not what he thinks he is saying. For example, I asked my daughter to tell me about an article she'd read about archeology, and she told me that she'd learned about all the important, overlooked discoveries that could be made from the mantle. Immediately, I pictured "mantle" as being the Earth's crust – which is why I got pretty confused until further probing led me to deduce that, "Oh! You mean a fireplace mantel!" She looked at me as if I were an idiot. Of course she'd been talking about objects dear to a family – on the mantel-place. But that's not at all what she was saying. That's why I have learned to act like a mirror, reflecting back what I am hearing and understanding, even if I know it's not what my son or daughter mean to say. In this way, they are learning to structure descriptions and conclusions in ways that escort readers and listeners, rather than leaving the message recipient to try to unpack what's written or said.

Essentially, I cannot implore more emphatically that teachers (and parents) practice avoiding the word "wrong." Case in point: last week, my five-year-old was at preschool, where the topic was opposites. His assistant teacher drew an arrow pointing up, and labeled it as such. He was to draw the opposite. So, carefully, he drew a horizontal line, and said, "Across." The appropriate response would have been to reply, "Hmmm. That's interesting. Why is 'across' the opposite of 'up'?" To which his answer would have been that horizontal is the opposite of vertical because they make perpendicular lines. Instead, he was told that he was "wrong," a declaration that had him worried to the point of tears later that night. Obviously, this is a kid who is bright enough to know what opposites are – and geometrically, he was absolutely right. By asking more questions rather than judging his answer, the teacher could have discussed that her point was what was the opposite direction of the arrow at the end of the line, and he would have said "down." He wasn't wrong. He was just missing the gestalt – the main idea – at the toenail of the matter, but technically, he was right. His only takeaway, though, was, "I was wrong." Similarly, when he asked why black and white were opposites, he didn't get an answer. "Why aren't black and green opposites, Mama?" he questioned me. I reminded him about black holes, devoid of all light and color. White light, though, as he'd seen with prisms and rainbows, could be "cracked" into the entire visible spectrum of colors. And suddenly, he shrugged his shoulders. "Yup," he said. "That makes sense. They *are* opposites." Feed them facts in logical arrangement, ask questions to help them make connections, and don't tell them they are simply wrong. It's quite possible they are more "right" than you are.

When it comes to the physical act of recording their thoughts, it is so important to act as the scribe, writing down what the Asperkid dictates; thus, the student doesn't have to worry about trying to fit his ideas in a thought bubble or on a particular line. Instead, the ideas can flow more naturally as the scribe records them. Alternatively, dictation software for mobile and desktop technologies abound – many for extremely reasonable prices. This won't produce the finished product or fill in bubbles or outlines, but as your Asperkid gets older and is expected to produce lengthier pieces, dictation software offers another way of easily translating thoughts into written words.

Regardless of whether the scribe is human or machine, someone will have to help that Asperkid "connect the dots," or fill in thought-process holes. In other words, explain that his ideas are great; now the reader wants even more (in the form of clarifying logical connections between ideas). Ask that child to be "redundantly" clear – to help "show" the reader their ideas. Besides the typical "who, what," and so on, specifically ask that the student think about perspective (this may be hard!) and mood (provide some possible choices). At first, the child may find this tedious; it will seem that whatever she envisions so, too, would her reader (there's the theory of mind catch). So try: tell me more about how x led to y. If this is so, then what must happen? What else? Be supportive of what's been written, never insulting of what is missing. Just like my little boy needed to be led onward from "I'm thirsty," your Asperkid may just need to be helped to give words to his own solutions.

There are amazing ideas swirling around the mind of that Asperkid of yours. Providing the right route for expression guarantees better academic achievement, and, more importantly, the chance for that child to show the world (and himself!) that he is a smart, capable person.

Solution summary: writing detours

- Rubber stamps
- Movable letters (magnets, wooden pieces, cards)

- Keyboarding
- Sorting cards
- Nomenclature cards
- Asking more questions to help connect ideas to expression
- Avoiding labeling thought patterns as "wrong"
- Dictation programs
- "Scribing"
- Visual organizers.

Conclusion

Watching a child struggle is a terrible thing. I've never felt angrier, more helpless, more fed up than when my children can't see how close to "getting there" they are just as they quit, explode, or implode. Like me, most parents and educators would give anything to help. And there is so much to try, even if some days, that simply means telling an Asperkid that you see how much potential she has within, even when she can't. Today, yet another mom of an Asperkid shook her head as I explained these processes for getting around writing problems. "I never would have thought of that in a million years," she said. Again, what had seemed intuitive to me just isn't, I guess. If that's the case, I can't begin to tell how privileged I am to help those who want to make the detours, but don't know where to turn for directions. Gas up – it's one heck of a ride.

5 LIVING THE PRACTICAL LIFE

Nothing is too obvious

One of my dear friends has a fantastic talent for interior design. She can walk into a room and see exactly what isn't working. Better than that, she can ask savvy questions to understand what the "vibe" *should* be, take a few measurements, spend a bit of time perusing the internet, and come up with the most spot-on, innovative plan for overhaul. For her, seeing what a space can be rather than what it is just comes naturally. I, on the other hand, couldn't be more untalented in that department. Put me in a home design store and I get completely distracted, lose direction, and generally mess up the whole project. Thank goodness she keeps showing up to save my poor house.

We all have people in our lives that complement who we are and who we aren't. Years ago, my mother said that we "use" each friend for a different purpose; not the best choice of words, but her message was actually true. The people we call "friends" each bring something special, something that is unique and distinct. If we were to populate our lives with folks just like us, with the exact same talents or gifts, we would all be terribly redundant and the world a lot worse off for the homogeneity.

Aspies, by our very natures, bring a little something different to the table. We add abilities, perspectives, and creations that no neurotypical ever could. On the other hand, there are a lot of skills we don't have naturally. I can write with the words simply rushing from my soul. I can design massively cool cakes with dry ice and sugar sculptures. But I cannot walk into a room and know how to make it work the way my friend does. And while the full scope of her natural talent will never be mine, I have learned enough by listening to her to start to be able to employ some of her strategies on my own. I recognize where I need help and am no longer mad at myself for failing to be the expert at everything.

Where others learn by "diffusion," we need explicit instruction. Like a teacher provides a textbook to study, those who help to raise Asperkids must offer lessons and primers in areas that seem perhaps obvious to neurotypicals. So allow me to speak on behalf of all Aspies when I tell you that there are some very real life skills that you have to teach us. I am truly uncertain where I missed some of these – like the idea that you have to rinse off dishes before putting them in the dishwasher, or how to correctly fold a T-shirt or towel. These I learned from a ticked-off housemate and a Martha Stewart show, respectively. Manners, I was certainly taught. Napkin in your lap, don't swear, say please and thank you. But when my mom would tell me to clean up my room, I truly had no clue how to begin. I went to college with lots of coins for the washing machine and no idea how to sort or correctly fold laundry. Balancing a checkbook, correctly cleaning the floors, polishing shoes, making a neat braid, maintaining appliances – all of these were foreign tasks that I certainly could approximate, but didn't really "own."

The issue isn't that my mother didn't have me pitch in (I was the official garden-weeder even in the middle of summer). No, my trouble was that just as I can't instinctively redecorate a room but can learn the basic principles, we Aspies need very clear, step-by-step instructions on how to manage jobs that are much more readily "picked up" by our neurotypical peers. Part of the problem may be our lack of focus or hyperfocus on the wrong thing, part may be problem-solving issues, part may be mindblindness – never really thinking about how that dish got cleaned or household got organized. No amount of frustration from parents, roommates, coworkers or friends will change the fact that without flowchart style how-to's, we won't do better and no one will feel better. We don't want to feel like bumbling failures at the mundane. To be totally honest, why we need the extra help isn't nearly as important to me as the fact that we *do* need the extra help – not to do something for us, but to show us (concretely!) how to do it for ourselves.

Aspies are often information junkies. As is typical for many of us, when I need to learn something, I read. A lot. A whole lot. There is really very little that one can't "study up on," given enough effort, and we're not talking just scholastics. My subscription to *Seventeen* magazine and the like was a conscious effort to literally learn everything I could about make-up, correct application, do's and don'ts. By the time I was a freshman in college, I had girls coming to my room to ask me to do their faces before dates or parties. These are lessons I am already teaching my daughter in bits and pieces now. Similarly, I taught myself how to bake by watching a million hours of *Food Network* and reading cookbooks, and then upped the ante by reading all I could about cake decorating; in six months I went from never having iced a cake to having a couture cake company featured on the cover of the business section of the newspaper. The same part of the brain that enjoys cataloging dinosaurs or Tudor history can find pleasure in the methodical collection and management of life skills. Approach us with strategies, facts, and lessons, not chores or corrections. Give us a model to follow and instructions on how to start, and we can amaze you.

How to begin: "helpful" grown-ups

As parents or teachers, therapists or caretakers, one of our greatest challenges is that we love being needed by our children, but know that it is our job to push greater and greater independence. At least, that's the usual experience. From the time their neurotypical kids are very young, moms and dads are already waging the inner battle between giving their little ones roots and helping them find their wings. The experience is a little bit different for the parents of Aspies. I clearly remember being at least nine, and my mom declaring it "the year Jenny will learn to make her own peanut butter and jelly sandwich." Obviously, she was ready for me to take a little bit more on for myself; yet she had never offered to teach me how to make the PB&J. More than likely, she presumed after sitting in a kitchen for so many years, of course I could make a simple sandwich. Maybe. I loved watching (OK, studying) cooking shows, and pretty soon could even whip up homemade breakfast syrups (putting my own spins on the recipe patterns I saw on television), but to be honest, I saw no reason to take on the challenge of the PB&J. I had never paid the process much attention, and there were plenty of other battles for me to figure out. So, my mom teased, cajoled, and scolded, but I don't think it ever occurred to her to teach me outright, support the process, and make it become my own.

I understand that. My five-year-old Asperkid takes an unbearably long time to change his clothes, and makes five trips back and forth from the dinner table to bring in his few dishes. My daughter forgets things every place she goes. Sometimes, I take a deep breath, help them go over the steps of a process out loud, and make it work together. Other times I just want to scream. But what I have learned is that unless pushed, Asperkids probably aren't going to attempt to take on new life skills. We're intimidated, maybe otherwise focused, but not lazy. That which is easy for you is so much more complicated to us. And when odds are that we are going to make a mistake, be publicly embarrassed, or annoy the people we love, there's not a whole lot of incentive to try.

Even in the most usual of circumstances, grown-ups who think they are being helpful will zip up jackets, tie shoes, and snap pants without being asked – perhaps they are impatient, perhaps they mean well. But in doing so, they stifle the child's motor planning, hand strength, hand-eye coordination, and organizational skills. Worse, they foil the Asperkid's much-needed journey toward self-confidence, an attribute only attainable through perserverance and eventual accomplishment. Contrarily, they may ask a child to perform a task without ensuring he has all the steps laid out in a way to which he can refer back. It's like sending him off in a sinking raft without a lifejacket.

The rule I ask you to go by is one I frequently state to extended family who visit: if the child has proper preparation for a task, please ___'t help him unless he asks you. Let him try first. And if he runs into trouble, this is the Asperkid's moment to learn to ask for help (something they are frequently uncomfortable doing – you may have to encourage this). At our house, kids learn early that if you want someone's help, you must go to the person you are addressing with anything they might need to assist you; screaming from another room is not going to work here, or anywhere else in the world. So we require a little bit of forethought, not to mention a dose of manners. Even then, we guide them, we don't take over. Slowly, an adult will describe the process while showing the steps needed for success. Coaching (on anything from sock folding to making change) may be broken down over several periods and repeated more than once for real mastery. That's OK. We're not looking for perfect! Success is the ability to cite a goal, enumerate the steps to get to that goal, and be able to retain and reenact the process independently.

Exercises of practical life: real-life skills at home and in school

In her work as a pediatrician and curriculum creator, Maria Montessori developed a curricular genre called "exercises of practical life," utilitarian activities introduced at the preschool and early elementary level. Superficially, they don't seem particularly relevant to academic success. Or perhaps they are quaint, but with a wink and a polite "thanks but no thanks," something parents and teachers might just as soon gloss over.

Big, whopping mistake. No matter how old or highly functional an Asperkid, tasks that seem menial and obvious to you, like sweeping a floor, washing the dishes, or polishing silver, are actually full of value in more ways than you imagine. Uncomplicated, everyday activities routinely carried out by others must be remedially, patiently taught. There is a lot of motor planning, organization, and multitasking that goes into almost every real-life skill – series of thoughts and executions that most neurotypical adults never even contemplate. Yet if we, like you, are to obtain some sense of mastery over the environment in which we study, live, and grow (the basis for most Aspie anxiety!), then we must be shown what to do and how to do it.

First, what precisely are "practical life activities?" Broken down, the name really does explain the concept: practical means purposeful, useful. Life, in this case, refers to the activities that are required for conducting a healthy, satisfying existence. Put them together, and the definition becomes clear. For any child – especially an Asperkid – a curriculum of thoroughly, patiently taught life skills is in no way remedial. On the contrary, Dr. Montessori's "exercises of practical life" is a series of real-world tasks that challenge and encourage the developing body and mind of most any child. For Asperkids in general, it can go far beyond that.

Initially, some of the activities seem antiquated – they were, after all, developed a century ago. But the finite nature of each, enhanced further by immediate gratification and tangible results, make flower-arranging, chopping veggies, or polishing a banister as satisfying for young people today. I have seen it first-hand. And it's why students like having "jobs" in school – even secondary students. Given a task and a domain to master, a child feels important, and seeks to shine.

In general, my layman's explanation of "practical life" would broadly sort tasks into personal grooming, polishing, pouring, transferring, textile work, woodwork, and housekeeping. However, the Association Montessori International (AMI) generally refers to Preliminary Exercises, Applied Exercises, Grace and Courtesy, and Control of Movement (www.infomontessori. com/practical-life/introduction.htm). Control of Movement is largely the gross motor work many Aspies are already tackling in occupational therapy.

Preliminary Exercises are the "basics," and focus on moving oneself or objects: folding, pouring, carrying without dropping things. However, adults who see our "clumsy" kids trying to navigate busy lab stations, cafeterias, and even family dinners know that none of those things are "basic." All the better that a loving, patient adult takes an unlimited amount of time to demonstrate and repeat any lesson as often as the child needs without judgment or commentary. How does your Asperkid close a door? I was sure doors all over our house were going to come crashing down. That is, until I literally took the time to conduct a full lesson on the subject. I showed my Asperkids how to reach out for the doorknob, turn the handle, close the door gently but firmly, and then, finally release the doorknob spring. Hallelujah! No more crashing or slamming (well, usually). Clear, modeled instruction, repeated a few times, and the idea stuck. What are the proper procedures for discreetly obtaining permission to get to the restroom?

Applied Exercises "apply" the motor planning, dexterity, focus and strength, skills mastered in preliminary work, to self-care and care of the child's environment. That would mean tasks like wiping up a spill successfully, sweeping under the table, or brushing one's hair. Preparing, serving, and cleaning up the daily snack (at home or in school) using appropriately sized kitchen tools is a fabulous way these applied skills can work their way into real-life situations. Trimming, cleaning, and arranging flowers requires scissor-work, patience, and a developing aesthetic appreciation – not to mention a full 25 steps or so to complete! Everything is difficult until it is simple, whether that be walking or long division.

Learning the art of "completing a process" when arranging flowers will impact appreciation for the environment, for other people's artistic contributions, for their work or living spaces, and, believe it or not, show itself in a student's willingness to thoroughly investigate and report upon a botanical life cycle. In my classes, I was willing to try anything, no matter how outrageous, if it reached my kids. I wish I had known then to pull out florist's foam and vases! Exercises such as using a mustard spoon to slowly transfer beans from one pretty china dish to another develop motor control and pencil grasp. Pouring rice between glass pitchers self-corrects hand-eye coordination; learning proper table setting introduces the topic of manners and public social skills, and could even lead to an investigation of table manners through the ages (you may not want to know about Tudor English mealtime nose-wiping advice, but I would bet a middle school or high school boy would!).

Break it down, man

Most everyone remembers the teacher's voice in the "Peanuts" cartoons. "Wah-wah-wah-wah," heard Charlie Brown. That's what an Asperkid hears when gobs of information are thrown at him. As long as an adult will take the time to break jobs down into steps, most any Asperkid can surprise those around him (including himself). No matter what the actual exercise, the adult must lead by example, breaking down every process from washing hands to arranging flowers to cutting wood or polishing shoes with methodical precision. Learning not to cut corners and to follow directions is at least half the battle. Learning to practice toward excellence even after a skill has been learned rudimentarily is another!

As with other materials, the child should always be set up for success, with adults pointing out errors only if really necessary. Make the exercise self-correcting. For example, as the nomenclature control cards allowed your Asperkid to acknowledge and correct his own errors, giving only the exactly right number of shirt hangers versus pants hangers will force him to double-back if he has one too few. Or explicitly tell him how to divide his class binder into colored tabs, and then put a matching colored marker dot on the top of any handout to help him get it to the right place on his own. No adult has to chastise him; instead, he is one step closer to owning a new life skill and to being a more independent learner.

If unsure about how, precisely, to dissect tasks that have become automatic to you, the Montessori Primary Guide website (available at www.infomontessori.com) gives some really clear examples to try. The North American Montessori Center even sells "practical life" manuals for children aged three through adolescence (see its website www.montessoritraining.net) that advance from simple hand washing procedures to skillfully wrapping a gift (also a great chance to discuss gift-giving etiquette or practice the math skills of shopping within a budget).

Each carefully selected endeavor is designed to be enjoyable purely on its own, but with the intended goal of helping the child gain muscle control and coordination, and develop confidence, generalize skill sets across locations, and feel more at ease in the neurotypical world.

Writes Montessori teacher Lesley Britton, for an adult, boring housekeeping tasks "have a purpose and are a means to an end – and the end result is more important than the process. Practical life activities enable the adult to control his physical and social environment." But for children, especially Aspies, the exact opposite is the case. "Performance of these simple daily routines is developmental and absorbing for the child; he is more interested in the processes involved than in the end result" (Britton 1992, p.22). In *Teach Me to Do it Myself*, Montessori teacher Maja Pitamic echoes that "these tasks may appear very simple because once mastered they are carried out automatically. But your child will experience a sense of accomplishment and self-worth when she is able to carry out these activities independently" (Pitamic 2004, p.13).

The most important thing Asperkids are learning is not really how to properly fold a towel or straighten a bookshelf (although they look awfully pretty!). It's more significant that they are developing dexterity and practicing following directions. Rather than simply hearing droning adult voices, they see for themselves that their efforts matter to the "team" (family or class) and that being patient and careful affect an outcome. Then, given an effective routine for employing these skills (keep reading for that!), they can avoid feeling overwhelmed, anxious, and frustrated. With the proper method, an overwhelming job – from getting dressed to managing an entire household – can be manageably broken into bite-sized pieces, and accomplished very successfully.

Ensure that each skill is taught one part at a time, making sure your Asperkid feels like an expert before challenging her with the next move. Give her "absorbent mind" time to soak up what you are teaching – a little bit at a time. Using real, weighty tools (dustpans, washboards) rather than pretend ones, you reinforce the import of her contribution to the family. Do not move too quickly; instead, break down every task into bite-sized steps that she can remember successfully and physically execute proficiently. From basic hygiene like properly washing hands and hair, to correct folding techniques (we love the FlipFold to subvert motor challenges and actually make the chore fun; see Resources), to delicate pouring, polishing and transferring exercises, the mastery of life skills means more than a tidier kitchen. It means pride, increased dexterity, enhanced concentration, improved sense of self, better coordination, and greater self-sufficiency. Let her repeat any activity as many times as she needs to feel capable and complete; it is how she learns.

Above all, the involved adult's goal must be to teach rather than to correct. Getting frustrated with a child's errors sends the message that his body, mind or both are disappointing and deficient. If something's not catching, the child may not be ready, or the lesson may have to change. Shorten sessions. Re-teach. Be patient. Congratulate the effort and the perseverance, no matter how long he lasted. Though it may first seem to you and to your Asperkid that there really isn't a great value in making a whole lesson out of correctly folding a T-shirt or towel, a century of practical life activities shows otherwise.

Taught in the privacy of the home or in quiet time with a caring professional, she will not compare herself to peers, and the process of learning becomes infinitely more powerful. From one task to the next, a child's concentration increases, impulsiveness can be calmed, orderly thought improves, and best of all, the Asperkid finally gets to feel the satisfactory rush of accomplishment. We want these Asperkids to grow into self-reliant, fully participatory citizens. Knowing that folks whom they love feel absolutely comfortable asking them to change toilet paper rolls, polish the good silver, or wash the real glass dishes says a lot to young people (no matter how brilliant!) about trust, self-worth, and the future.

The practical classroom

Right now, teachers operating in traditional school settings may be wondering how any of this "practical life" mumbo jumbo plays out for them. Unlike in the Montessori classroom or in the home, Sock-Folding 101 is not on the usual school agenda, although primary teachers may find great benefit in "standard" performance by increasing foundational skills in nontraditional ways. Adding some mirror polishing might be worth a try over yet another handwriting drill. I implore you *not* to think for a moment that this "practical life" bean pouring, dustpan using stuff does not apply to "regular" school. Try it, and the evidence will speak for itself.

Beyond motor control and task completion, Aspies have more to gain from learning "practical" skills at school. A lot more. Organization, taught systematically, can become a habit even at an early age. We've explored that already. Conversely, disorganization, not undone early, can also become a habit. Someone who wants to speak Swahili but has never studied it is hardly about to speak it fluently tomorrow. An Aspie, not overtly taught how to manage her learning environment, is just about as likely to succeed.

One afternoon, my daughter showed me her homework sheet from school. It was torn, and rather rumpled, neither of which sat well with me. Importantly, she, like most Aspies, didn't understand that messy schoolwork conveyed a lack of effort on her part; that it sent a message aside from her actual answers to the math problems. To her, what mattered was the accuracy of her responses, and that was it. But to a teacher (or later, an employer or client), it said that she couldn't really be bothered, had better things to do, or didn't take much pride in herself – none of which was the case. So, my first response was to explain how presentation affects reception and perception. We're still working on that.

The next issue was how the paper had gotten so bruised in the first place. When asked, she admitted that her desk was "a little messy," which was why the paper had been damaged. Knowing the enduring battle in her bedroom, I could only imagine what was going on in that desk! So, I sent the teacher a brief email asking her to help my daughter cull through her things. Here lies important point number one: a child's workspace is her launch pad for learning. As a well-made bed at home sets a mood, so does a disheveled locker, cubby, or desk. And that mood is panic.

Imagine peering into a desk or locker that is a mass of paperwork, broken crayons, random playground bits, or accumulated jackets, and trying to complete a task before the period bell rings or the next step in an explanation is missed. It means that the student – who already has to try to organize his thoughts amidst a noisy, bright, distracting environment, grab the right supplies, and keep up with peers – is doomed to failure before he even begins. Messy locker or desk equals missed directions, disorganized work, lowered self-esteem, lessened initiative, and depressed learning. Not to mention that it's embarrassing.

So what to do? Here is the practical "school life" lesson. I have frequently observed that telling any of my children to "tidy your room" guaranteed me one of two results – a blank stare, or a determined little person who disappeared with conviction, only to get lost along the way in some odd toy or some tangential (and nonessential) subtask. Blanket directive wrought incomplete task, frustrated mom, and defensive or self-loathing Asperkid.

Why? Virtually every Aspie has some degree of attention deficit disorder (with or without hyperactivity: ADD/ADHD), even if they (or their parents or school) don't know it. Personally, while I was diagnosed with Aspie a year ago, I didn't realise I had ADD until six months later. During one session, I joked to my own adult psychiatrist about my super-high coffee intake. After some objective, quantitative testing, it turns out that I did, indeed, have significant ADD, and that I'd been self-medicating with caffeine for years. As the doctor commented, he could only imagine what I could have accomplished had I known as a young person. So, even if a student's record doesn't indicate that she has ADD/ADHD, if she has Asperger's, just assume she does. Why? My daughter got an "Excellent" for "Listens to Directions" on her report card. Yet she received a "Needs Improvement" for following them. She's not noncompliant. She got distracted. And, the teacher reported to me, sometimes the entire class would be lined up ready to march to some other locale, while my daughter was still at her desk, working on a previous task and unaware that she was missing anything. There's your hyperfocus on one thing, and blaring lax elsewhere. If we want our Asperkids to succeed, we have to direct them differently than we do our other students.

Giving a blanket directive to "clean up" will not work. Many teachers, with wonderful intent, even provide class time for their students to tidy their workspaces. For an Asperkid, that means lack of specific guidance in a room full of visual and auditory stimuli (kids laughing, papers flying). Progress just isn't going to be made. Or, alternatively, the Asperkid will begin, but lose himself in arranging his pencils perfectly or righting some ill-fitting folders, and find his time allotment gone with little to nothing done.

When I contacted the teacher on the afternoon of the torn paperwork, she took a quick gander and was, apparently, shocked at the level of chaos in such a small space. Needless to say, I wasn't. Everything is an extreme with an Aspie.

The key to the "practical life" skills in desk or locker maintenance begins with a private, quiet opportunity – before school, after, by appointment. Teacher (or counselor) and student should evaluate the workspace without judgment or reprimand, and (using a timer to make it a finite, non-overwhelming project), together first, tackle supplies, texts, assignments, and homework in bite-sized bits.

From there on out, use clear, short-worded directions provided both in writing and orally. For example, Monday may be "Writing Implement Day," and might feature an index-card-sized, reusable reminder that reads: "Pencils, 3. Sharpen. Pens, 2. Check ink. Highlighters, 2; no cap = throw away." Read it aloud, ask the Asperkid to repeat it back (to check for comprehension), and then hand it to him to use as a memory aide (he should return it to you upon completion). Reward participation and task completion initially, then phase that out with increasing independence becoming its own prize.

Routinely issued deck/locker/cubby check-ins should occur for upkeep, rather than overhaul. That doesn't mean every so often – we're talking perhaps daily or maybe every other day, gauging the child's level of emotional energy. This is tough for her, so if she's worn or prickly, the result will not be an empowered Asperkid who is learning how to supplement deficient executive functioning, but a frazzled, tired, meltdown. Use a sticker chart or Lego, whatever works as frequent motivation; if the Asperkid's special interest is known (which it will be by most anyone who spends time with him), try to involve that in the way expectations are phrased. It really *will* make a difference.

Some other important tips:

- A place for everything and everything in its place. I am a big advocate of the Desk-a-Doo for aiding elementary students (available online at www.deskadoo.com), and adjustable locker shelves for older kids. Compartmentalize. Make large, open storage into smaller, more manageable segments.

- Sort everything (by color per subject, or by morning versus afternoon class). Label. Be overly obvious and embrace your label-maker.

- Give very specific directions on how long paperwork is expected to be kept, and when it should be thrown away. With our OCD tendencies, Aspies are notorious pack-rats. Be aware that the student may be afraid of being penalized for throwing things away.

- Put stickers near the top of the front, back and spine of folders or binders. This will give the Asperkid a visual reminder as to which way is "up," and help avoid embarrassing spills in crowded halls.

More advanced practical life tasks, called "Grace and Courtesy" in Montessori lingo, echo the manners every involved adult (parents and teachers) must teach Asperkids so that they can function in a neurotypical world; the problem is, again, that Asperkids need to learn social skills a little differently. A young Aspie who politely corrects his teacher, insisting that he can't put away his coat as he only has a rain jacket, may end up being ejected from class in confused tears if "courtesy" is the only barometer. This actually happened to my four-year-old son in a special education class. But as anyone familiar with Asperger's knows, he wasn't being rude, he was being precise, and doesn't yet really know how to hold back an unnecessary correction. This same little guy was stripped of playtime in preschool for not following teacher directions on how to perform an art task; truth be told, he was utterly confused, and needs to repeat directions back to his instructors (and mom) before even beginning to be sure he understands what's expected of him.

In order to make a lesson really stick, an Asperkid has to be told the logic behind said activity, and how it benefits him. For example, I had a conversation with my daughter last night about saying thank you to people, and how sometimes Aspies had a hard time noticing when others were actively showing love. After a two-day hospital admission, she'd wanted to stay longer when discharge finally came. The reason? She liked a video game they had – the idea that the lives of her parents, grandmother, and two brothers were all in a good bit of chaos never even occurred to her. So, we came up with another short-and-sweet coaching guide:

1. *Notice* folks around you.

2. *People being nice* to you are choosing to show you love.

3. If that makes you feel good, *tell them*, so they know it mattered.

4. Short version: *Notice people being nice. Tell them.*

That line of thought seems obvious to most, but not to a mindblind Aspie who isn't arrogant; she just never even realized that others were choosing to be with her, rather than doing activities of their own preference.

The practical (home) life: "wash on Monday, mend on Tuesday..."

Previously, we discussed the importance of a "prepared environment" in which everything the child uses is accessible and sized for her. I can't stress enough how important that is, especially for our Asperkids in school *and* at home! When we designed my daughter's bedroom, we bought a fabulous bed with a trundle underneath. It was gorgeous, tall, and lush. But the kid can't make this bed to save her life. She's tiny, and there is just no way for her to have a positive experience learning to change sheets or straighten a comforter on a bed that is too tall and cumbersome. That would be setting her up to fail. We learned from that mistake; when her younger brother was ready to move out of his toddler bed, we bought him a bed (from Ikea) that is, well, short. He can walk around it easily and reach every corner. The kids also have smaller-sized laundry baskets (see the "For Small

Hands" website in Resources) that they can maneuver without help. This is a platform for success and pride.

Years ago, I invested in what we affectionately call "The Tower." It's not an exaggeration to say that it is one of the most important pieces of furniture in our home. Properly named "The Learning Tower," this is, essentially, a movable, guard-railed, elevated platform that at least two small children can use at a time (see the "For Small Hands" website in Resources). By standing on it, the kids are active participants in our family life – not undersized onlookers. Cooking, home repair, washing dishes, and a million other jobs that would otherwise be outside of their reach are easily within their grasp.

From The Tower, the kids have taken on a new responsibility: dinner dishes. While yes, part of that job is about lightening Mom's load, it was really a clandestine lesson in teamwork – not exactly an Asperkid specialty. Initially, there was a lot of bossing and shouting; it was not pretty, I tell you. So, Daddy had a solution: a three-legged hour. With one leg each tied to their sibling's, like at a Field Day race, the two older kids had to do everything together for an hour – and had to communicate better to avoid falling over! And yes, Dad was present the whole time. His best idea was to even out the playing field a little by putting our more passive five-year-old in charge of his usually dominant big sister – the perfect forum to practice both speaking up and listening, respectively. At the end of the exercise, they were up on The Tower washing and laughing. Yes!

For the actual task of dishwashing, they use light plastic bins, a small-handled, easily gripped brush, and cloth towels, following an explicit process of scrubbing, rinsing, and drying that I taught by showing and telling over a few days; after the dishes are clean, damp cloths go into their own laundry basket. When it gets full, the kids are then in charge of laundering them, too. One child dibs and rubs the towels on an old-fashioned scrub board (a secret tool for developing upper-body strength and rhythm, both of which affect writing skills!), then the other rinses and uses clothes-pins (fine motor work and hand strengthening) to clip them to dry on an old-fashioned, child-sized clothes rack. Dexterity, planning, turn-taking, communication, pride in work and clean dishes – all because of child-sized tools and clearly explicated instructions.

To further encourage mastery over their environment, I sectioned off one low-positioned cabinet shelf for the children's snacks, plastic bowls, and child-sized food preparation tools. There is a small, wooden cutting board, a vegetable-cutter designed "For Small Hands" (see Resources), and little "spreaders," each lying out on clean kitchen towels. Because the objects are small and are clearly displayed, they meet the kids' physical needs as well as psychological ones – my Asperkids know, at a much younger age than I did, that they can successfully and safely participate in their home; they are expected to take on new jobs and responsibilities because we *know* they can be successful (full tanks of gas and time to get there). Our line, which they can repeat, is, "Mom and Dad will never ask me to try something until they have given me everything I need to do it right." Methods, tools, and support, they have it all, and have developed much more self-respect as a result.

Practical life exercises are available in most every Montessori book I have mentioned and on most of the websites, too. While some special materials are helpful because of their size, just remember to focus on the process rather than the perfect outcome – mopping, crumbing a table, polishing Daddy's shoes, setting the table, pouring increasingly less dense substances, window washing, sanding and hammering and wood. These are all about acquiring real-world skills and developing a sense of self within the group.

In the first Little House book, Laura Ingalls Wilder recalls a rhyme her mother sang. "Wash on Monday, mend on Tuesday..." it began. The intent was to help children remember whatever special job, aside from everyday tasks, had been designated per day. And though it was listing work, the little pioneer sisters enjoyed it because they knew what was coming, and because it gave them a unified sense of pride and purpose. I loved that list. Most Asperkids really would; it is logical, organized, and complete. And it's a schedule. Those rock.

If a parent has endeavored to teach their Asperkid sock pairing, mirror polishing, and dishwasher loading, but has no system for seamlessly employing those skills into the home life, what he has is CHAOS. This is a term that I quote affectionately from one of my favorite websites, Marla Cilley's FlyLady.net. "C.H.A.O.S.," the site explains, stands for "Can't Have Anyone Over Syndrome." It's what happens when disorganization and perfectionism meet – and it isn't pretty.

While the FlyLady homepage is an absolute assault of information, I have yet to find a better, more encouraging system for managing a home. Most importantly, the site touches on everything from cleaning toilets to financial "decluttering" to exercise, in a way that will not allow followers to be derailed by perfectionism or put off overwhelming tasks. Knowing Aspies, those two points are at least half the battle. Perhaps that's why, even if our ADD is getting the better of us, the plan's "baby steps" are exactly what Aspies need to feel successful immediately. Readers are told "jump in where you are," that they are "not behind, [but] just getting started," and "you can do anything for 15 minutes." That's just the kind of encouragement any family of an Aspie (and the Aspie herself) needs.

Whatever system works best for your family is grand. Martha Stewart's website lists a bevy of homekeeping checklists and tips (www.marthastewart.com). So does the magazine *Real Simple* (www.realsimple.com). It doesn't matter which system you choose to follow. Just be sure to choose one, because after you have taken the time to teach your Asperkid "useful activities of practical life," he has to know what to do with those skills. The simple truth is that the more routinized (read: automatic) your home, the less anxiety producing it is for your Asperkid, the more likely he will be able to anticipate and successfully execute his household chores, and the more positive the environment for everyone.

You will recall that I explained how, in order to succeed at most new tasks, Aspies need a model (person or object) to watch and study, and explicit directions of how to complete the process. The last piece is a clear schedule and method by which to employ those skills. You (or FlyLady, or Martha or even a grandparent!) are the child's model, and practical life skills as explicated by Montessori books and websites, magazines like *Real Simple* or books like *Martha Stewart's Homekeeping Handbook* (2006) make excellent step-by-step how-to's. My preference for FlyLady is due to her method of applying those skills in a predictable, accessible way. Daily work relies heavily on routine (how Aspie-friendly!), practical strategies for attacking clutter (the anti-prepared environment), avid use of social media, apps, online reminders during the day (techno-fab), all wrapped up in a simple, effective, orderly system. We Aspies love our systems. And routines.

Essentially, the FlyLady method divides a home into designated weekly "zones": the living room, the main bathroom, and so on. In addition to daily morning and bedtime routines, surprise daily missions assign finite zone-specific jobs (using timers). Whether flinging unmatched plastic lids, sweeping the front steps, or clearing off a single flat surface, these little tasks break giant-sized demands into something doable.

FlyLady is meant for the adult in charge of the home. But, now you've seen other not-quite-right strategies tweaked and modified to beautifully fit the age and skill set of our Asperkids, the same approach can "fly" for FlyLady (or Martha, etc.). Our five- and eight-year-olds have clear charts illustrating their morning and bedtime routines which, as mentioned before, feature their special interests. Each poster pictorially instructs the child to get dress/undressed, put soiled clothes in the hamper, put away any clean laundry that has been left by Mom, and to brush hair/teeth. That's it – whether directing activity in the dinosaur den or the demigod camp cabin, the images are few, vivid and carefully matched to the child.

Whether at home or in school, basic organizational and practical life skills can garner a better response when put in terms of the passion. We've explored that idea as per classroom use. What about at home?

Keeping my daughter's room even vaguely tidy has been a lifelong losing battle. And I do mean battle. We've used every sticker chart and token system known to humankind and failed. I've tried to pare down the clutter, break tasks into digestible parcels, used plastic zip baggies to sort and make things visible, but the consistent response has been exasperation, frustration, and outright anger, until I figured a way to tie everything in to her beloved book series and ancient mythology. Then, eureka!

We exchanged the "run of the mill" getting-ready routine chart for one that features bright graphics which are directly related to her passion. One 20-minute session, a Google search or two, and I could cut and paste public domain or fan art onto a simple-to-follow wall chart. Let's look at a "generic" version of a reoccurring chore, and pose it next to the "special interestified" one I created for my daughter. Even if your Asperkid's passion is frogs or dogs or trains, you can apply the strategy. The intention is the same, if not the appearance or language of the final product. The general idea begins as shown in the illustration.

Information to be presented on page	Generic version	Special interest version (example: Greek mythology)
Purpose of chart	Daily routine	Daily demigod cabin check
Set the scene	Photo of child's room	Online fan art drawing of Greek demigods' summer camp from book series
Get dressed	Photo of a favorite outfit	Photo of demigod camp T-shirt for sale online

Our older Asperkid also has a daily "zone" to attend to in her room; essentially, it's just a strategy for keeping the room tidy throughout the week, so there is never a point where she has to go in and try to salvage a mess that is really beyond her organizational capabilities. Each day has its own page in a reminder binder, clearly showing what must be straightened; no wiggle room is left for ambiguity, dispute, or confusion. Each week is cyclical, with the room's "zones" predictable and repeating. In this way, our Aspergirl has a plain account of how and when she should use the practical life skills she's learning, and knows that whatever is asked of her will be concise and totally doable.

The FlyLady's routine-driven, timer-bound system of dividing room-keeping into small daily tasks remains (e.g. Monday is the bed area – putting away strewn books, empty cups on the nightstand, loose pajama bits); it is outlined for reference in a binder with clear expectations and an emphasis on quick, symbolic cues rather than blathering instructions. The example shown is Friday's page. My goal was to get her to address her vanity area, a certain bastion for clutter. On that day, my Aspergirl was to spend no more than ten minutes tidying and decluttering the area around her vanity, putting away jewelry, hair accessories, and lipsticks. So, what information did I need to convey, and how to phrase it?

Information to be presented on page	Generic version	Special interest version (example: Greek mythology)
Day name	Friday	Aphrodite's Mirror
Main graphic	Calendar square or simply the word, "Friday"	Botticelli's *Birth of Venus*, the classical personage of Friday's namesake
Visuals of items to be managed/ tidied	Photographs (minimum number)	Images of: jewelry, hair accessories, and lipsticks

After some tweaking, the final page in the binder looks like the illustration on the following page.

Friday: Aphrodite's Mirror

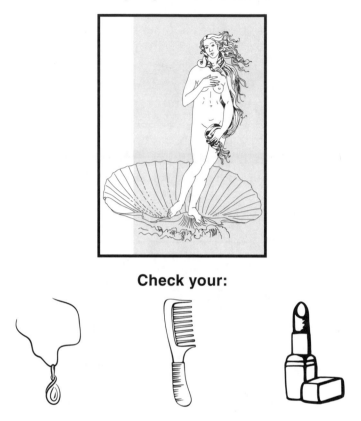

Check your:

Other days are similar. On "Library of the Acropolis" Day, she is to look around her room for any "parchments" (aka books) that may have migrated, and replace them to her bookcase. And while your Asperkid's Friday may not feature a clip art cut-and-paste Botticelli painting, you get the drift. Make it his/her own.

Beyond the routine, every day also offers an optional bonus challenge, a "tweaked" version of mini-"challenges" issued regularly by a super Facebook group called "FlyLady Kelly: Giving Your Children Wings." This task is a surprise, and it's how my eldest earns "stars" (or stickers or what have you) toward a larger, 30-day prize. For Asperkids, the regularly published Facebook challenges need to be altered somewhat – they must be finite (all have time limits), uber-concise, engaging, and dynamic. And again, it is more effective to lay out an original, special-interest-worded version of that daily challenge.

Very importantly, I choose to post bonus tasks which are specifically invented to bring my daughter out of her room into the larger "home team" domain where her efforts benefit those other than just herself. Only occasionally do they focus solely on her space in the home, more often emphasizing her important role in our family as a whole, and distancing her from a "that's not my job" mentality. How does it work? Let's use that comparison of generic versus "special-interest-tweak" method (I've included one "in your room" task to give an idea of something that would be too long to include in daily maintenance).

Generic version	Special interest version (example: Greek mythology)
Tidy someone else's mess/ maintain overall home environment	Pick up and return ten spears, lyres, or similar items left around by fellow Olympians
Help Mom fold laundry/cook dinner, etc.	Assist Hestia, Goddess of the Home and Hearth, with her domestic duties for ten minutes
Pick up fallen clothing or loose hangers from bedroom closet floor	Five-minute Chiton Check: replace any chitons which may have fallen to the floor and return stray hangers to chiton chamber

The final product is a (silver, glittery) master poster entitled, "Athena's Strategy of the Day In the Battle Against Chaos." Underneath that headline and a photograph, there is a Velcro dot stuck in the middle of a large, blank space. While the poster stays up on her bedroom wall all the time, "Athena's" specific "strategies" can be easily changed. As often as I like, I can peel off and tack up new (carefully-phrased) challenges, sticking them right onto the Velcro spot beneath Athena's gaze (see illustration).

Athena's Strategy of the Day

In the Battle Against χάος

Today's Strategy:

Good As Gone

No one can become wise amidst junk! So...

Get a **garbage bag**.

Empty your trash can into the bag.

Toss the bag into the harpies' rubbish bin

(cleverly disguised as the garbage can out back).

A blank space below the image has a Velcro dot where I can stick a new challenge daily (or as I can remember!).

All of the charts have few, carefully chosen words, specific numbers/times/locations, lots of white space and engaging visuals.

Proof that this works? My husband's latest fascination is the science fiction series "Stargate SG:1." And guess what ringtone he selected on his iPhone as the "reminder" alarm, rather than the "irritating" built-in sound? The show's theme song. Even for Asper-adults, everyday life is more doable when tied to the special interest. My daughter reminds me that sparkly silver glitter paper doesn't hurt, either.

After a month of blending carefully laid-out practical life skills, routines for making them more manageable, and reframing them in terms of special interest, things were profoundly different. Beyond a prize earned, her attitude toward pitching in was profoundly changed – finally, we saw a willingness to accept the helpful domestic reminders without seeing them as demeaning. Does she suddenly *love* doing chores? No, but who does? The big deal is that she is tolerating tedious tasks that she'd otherwise turned into ugly power struggles; and while yes, her laundry still winds up on the floor sometimes... She. Is. Doing it.

Usually.

6 DEAR SANTA, I'D LIKE A FRIEND FOR CHRISTMAS

OK, the honest truth is that when I wrote to Santa, asking for a friend for Christmas, I'm not sure who the intended audience actually was. Might've been the big guy. Might've been my parents – I did know they'd read it before mailing it off, after all. What I really do know is that I actually did write to Santa asking for a friend for Christmas, and that totally breaks my grown-up heart.

This is the really tough stuff. Universally, social guffaws are the primary commonality in diagnosing Asperger's – yet just tonight, a girlfriend who knows I have Asperger's called me "social." It's funny. I've told my daughter many times that what we perceive about people is what they exude, not necessarily what they are. Asperger's is no different. As a kid, I lay on tropical beaches reading near the volleyball net. My family went on annual holidays to the Caribbean, where I had absolutely no clue how to blend in and have fun. Plus the whole redhead/pale skin combination didn't really bode well with equatorial sun. So, I plugged my ears with headphones and lost myself in books, happy to look as though I had a legitimate excuse to be too busy to get involved. So not the case. I just had no idea what to say or do, so I buried myself in fiction. Until, years later, I had lines and scripts to memorize and flirtations (meant for the stage) to practice and hone. Suddenly, affectation was a benefit.

Adolescence is not a pretty thing in the best of circumstances. It's why, when I chose to teach middle school, parents often joked that I was either crazy-brave or masochistic. Neither was true. I just knew that's where I was needed. Above any curricular or practical goal, I believe that every teacher, counselor, parent, and caregiver has a part to play in showing Aspies what we need to do to compensate for that which our brains are just not hardwired to do otherwise. I don't care how superbly you teach math, develop sensory integration, or cook your kids' favorite dinner, if a child is lonely, every other aspect of his life (and yours, too) suffers.

On the contrary, an adult who takes the time to notice a need can save a young heart. Back in that miserable seventh grade year of mine, that is exactly what happened to me. My middle school had a program called "Advisor/Advisee" (AA), a weird name with a good intention. Basically, it was a regular time when students and teachers put away textbooks to discuss the issues endemic to adolescence: peer pressure, drugs, and so on. For the most part, I'm guessing it felt like a colossal waste of time to the majority of students and teachers involved. Sort of like a live, mandatory after-school special. But for me, something sort of amazing happened.

Unlike most kids, who were assigned to "talking groups" with our main teachers (in my case, that would've put me right back in the "Ding, dong, the witch is dead" crew), I somehow managed to get "assigned" to the music teacher (whom I loved). Mrs. Silbert just seemed to sense that I needed some serious lifelines thrown my way. So, without any official fanfare, she simply and casually extended "AA" into the following period, lunch. Besides myself, three other students, a new girl I enjoyed, a *Star Trek*-loving shy guy, and a popular football player, stayed, too. Though there were times in years to come that we each disappointed one another, we became more than just good friends – we became family, giving phone tips on what to do (or not to do) in social situations, broadening social circles. Heck, I even took one of the guys for a make-over and we two girls taught him to dance. Families vacationed together, and years later, we were attending (or actually being part of) one another's weddings. Even Mrs. Silbert, the teacher who created our "Breakfast Club" of sorts, was tearing up the dance floor at mine. She changed my life, plain and simple.

Aspies don't need crowds of friends; we need one or two really good ones. Quality not quantity. That's why the buddy system is the last, but absolutely most essential ingredient, to "practical" in-school solutions. At home, Asperkids (and even some adults) rely on a parent to serve as personal assistant. They're not "using" us, they are legitimately in need. In school, there is also a very real need for a trusted guide, but all too often, teachers view dependence upon another student as inadequacy. It isn't.

When I attended my daughter's parent/teacher conference, only to be surprised by the news that she was being "demoted" for social reasons, one of the main points the teacher made was how heavily my Aspergirl relied upon another child to tell her where to go and what to do. Make no mistake – this wasn't about being a pushover. Blind kids need seeing-eye dogs. My child needed a seeing-eye friend who could navigate the social and organizational worlds that completely eluded her. Rewind 20 years, and I had needed the same thing. Listen to Dr. Tony Attwood or Dr. Jed Baker (Attwood 2010; Baker 2010), who advocate the purposeful selection by school staff of a confident, intelligent, well-liked, understanding "buddy" to accompany an Asperkid through class transitions, physical education class, recreation time, academic choices, social minefields, and so on. My daughter had naturally found her buddy (who, by the way, enjoyed that role), but the school frowned upon the need. At age 35, I can look back and profess honestly that I can't imagine my life without Mrs. Silbert and her ahead-of-the-times solution for an awfully lonely kid. How sad that 20 years later, the same support might be denied to those who need it.

Teachers are asked to do so much, I know. And this is just one more thing. All I can say is that I do not think I can possibly overstate the importance of seeing the humanity of those young people before you in the desks or hallways. And so, I completely credit Mrs. Silbert, and teachers like her, for making me into the teacher I became – both of my own children and of those in my schoolroom, and for any good I wrought. Just last night, I received an unsolicited message on Facebook from a former student; now a young adult, she was once a closed-off adolescent whom I only got to teach for six weeks. "I was looking at my old 6th grade year book," she wrote, "and I saw the message you wrote in mine. The quote stood out, 'Still waters run deep.' ...I looked forward to your class. I had a rough middle school experience but some good came out of it because I did meet you." My reply to her message was instant and certain, "The best for you is yet to come." And I believe that is true.

Because let's be honest. Kids can be, forgive my bluntness, like sharks – they smell blood in the water. A child who is desperate for friends is that wounded swimmer, vulnerable and exposed. I am still not sure whether adults lose that instinct, or simply bury it. Maybe it depends on the individual, but even the schoolmate who told me to kill myself daily in high school has sent jovial "hello's" online, and even asked me out during our college years. Perhaps it's selective memory. I don't know. It is, however, why I issue this cautionary warning.

Even the "highest functioning" (awful term!) Asperkid is not as adept at social nuance as her neurotypical peers. It's one of the reasons Asperkids tend to function best socially around older children (who may guide or nurture them) and younger kids (who will allow themselves to be bossed). Immediate peers are, by far, the toughest. This is why I have to say that the best thing we ever did for our middle son was to start him in primary school a year later, and let him be the oldest in his preschool classes. Among kids just a tad younger, he is popular; he is admired for his intellect and leadership, traits that came across as professorial and dictatorial with children of exactly the same age.

However, in the world of "mean girls" and television exposés on bullying, I have watched my daughter try to keep up with other kids. As one observer confided in me, "She is their grunt." And it's true. She does the "go-fer-ing" for any supplies anyone might need, willing to do whatever it takes to be included. That terrifies me for the more complicated years to come. It's also why I have been very honest with her about my opinion of the way particular children treat others, both critically and complimentarily. And I am asking, though I don't know how clearly she can or will hear me, that she trust our call on which kids are "worth her energy" to make and maintain as friends. Much as my youngest doesn't yet understand the dangers of crossing a street and therefore must rely on our guidance, for right now, we have explained, there are dangers of which she, too, is unaware.

Aspies make loyal friends. We're not always attentive, but we are always true blue. The problem is that we expect the rest of the world to be the kind of friends we would be in return. We think, naively, that other people's intentions are as pure as our own. We are oblivious to hidden agendas or manipulation. It is our biggest weakness – we can't see another's perspective, so we cannot imagine they would want to hurt us, when all we want is to be friends.

Parents, you have a job, too, and it may not be what you think. I have watched well-intentioned parents sit back, happy that their child has *any* friends at all, no matter the quality of the others' characters. I have also witnessed parents try to "buy" friends for their Asperkids by throwing the coolest parties or planning superfun playdate activities. I may have been guilty of the latter myself. Heck, I've even seen my mother try to help her granddaughter by "setting up" friendships and pen-pals. But our little girl doesn't possess the drive or empathy to maintain those relationships, built largely on a false, neurotypical persona "created" (though lovingly) by her grandmother. In the end, everyone (including the other child) is let down.

"Faking it" or engineering inclusion only leaves an Asperkid believing that without pretense, no one would choose to be his or her friend. And that, I can tell you, is a terrible place to be – and is totally opposite of what the family members are trying to create. It may take longer for an Asperkid to make a real, true friend than others. That's hard to watch, I know; it's harder to live. Childhood, for Aspies, is like a time we mostly wish we could all simply skip over. But it has to be real to count.

Instead of putting on a "show," invest that time and energy in teaching your Asperkid to match her volume, energy level or demeanor to one or two other kids'. In other words, pay attention to the action in the room. If you finish a test ahead of everyone else, don't draw attention to yourself. The other kids aren't going to be impressed – they are going to be put off (guilty, right here). If no one else is being silly or bouncing around, then it's probably not cool for you to be quite so hyper, either. Help them by pointing out specific tricks – sitting next to someone else who is alone, or noticing the clothing trends in magazines. Your Asperkid may not care to be connected – and if he or she is truly more content that way, fine. But don't be fooled by insecurity masked as nonchalance. Offer the tips anyway. The Aspie has the choice to take them or not. Make specific suggestions in positive ways (as opposed to, "Don't x, y, or z!"), and be there to listen – not always advise.

Years ago, I taught my daughter a trick that she has used ever since. She was trying to do a maze, and kept getting mixed up or lost. I showed her that if she put her finger at the end and traced her way back, she'd know exactly where to draw her line before she ever put pencil to paper. "Isn't that cheating?" she asked. Absolutely not. In life, we need to know where we are headed in order to make the choices and plans that will take us there. As the young heroine's father reminds his daughter in Disney's *The Princess and the Frog* (2009), wishing on the star only gets you so far. The rest comes from hard work. The other evening was a bad one around here. My daughter has been feeling lonely, and has been acting out – then feeling regretful for her words or actions. She was tearful, and didn't know what to do. So, we talked about a point down further in the maze of her life. What was it that she could focus on instead of the here and now, and what could she do to get there? Time was going to pass either way; she could choose to spend it lost in the sorrow of one point on the journey, or focused on the proud moments to come. I know her "right now" is hard. I know it from the bottom of my soul, and I cannot change it. What I can do, though, is give her power, a power I never knew I had. That is, we can make our students, sons, and daughters aware of their power to actively choose the attitude they will take each morning.

There is a parable, whose author is unknown, which perfectly summarizes my view of the world. It tells of a woman who awakes to find only three hairs on her head. She smiles and says, "I think I'll braid my hair today." The next day, she discovers only two hairs, and gladly proclaims that today, she will part her hair down the middle! On the third morning, she spies one hair left, and laughs, "I will wear a ponytail today!" And when at last she wakes to find no hairs remaining, she joyfully announces, "Yay! I don't have to do my hair today!" Life begins at the edge of our comfort zones, I have heard. And if that's the case, that is the whole world for us Aspies. I guess that means we Aspies have a lot of living to do.

7 IT DEPENDS ON WHERE YOU'RE STANDING

Perspectives on Comfort Zones

Have you ever read C.S. Lewis's *The Magician's Nephew* (1955)? I mean, most folks know about Narnia, and the tales of the kids through the wardrobe. But are you familiar with the lesser known prequels? They put everything to come in motion and perspective – explaining the magic and the allegorical adventures ahead. As in most of life, there's more to the story than we think we know. That is the power of perspective. It tags question marks where we think there are periods, undoes absolutes. As Lewis put it perfectly, "what you see and hear depends a good deal on where you are standing: it also depends on what sort of person you are" (Lewis 1955, p.137). And if you are an Aspie sort of person, your perspective is generally a little bit different.

I got glasses when I was seven years old. A routine physical had shown that I was quite significantly nearsighted, yet my parents hadn't noticed, and neither had I. In retrospect, I thought I could see as far as everyone else could. Apparently, that wasn't the case. Double-checking the doctor's exam, my mom tested me herself at, of all places, a Disney on Ice show. She asked me to read a blinking sign across the arena, and no, of course I couldn't! Turned out, I should've been able to – I never realized that the way I saw the world was any different. To me, my own eyesight seemed normal. Such is perspective. Until we stand in another's shoes – or wear their glasses

– we don't know what they see that we don't, and vice versa. I would guess that I can't even imagine the keen eyesight of a deaf person, or the intensified sense of touch of a blind child reading Braille.

What I am getting at is that in most every way, the Aspie experience is different than the usual life. It's not worse or better, just different. But as I normalized my nearsightedness, we Aspies don't recognize our perspective as unique until you give us something to compare it against. It's that mindblindness again. To imagine the ways your neurotypical mind works is almost as impossible for me as it is for you to stand where I am. Consequently, it is a lifelong journey of introspection that allows Aspies to identify the distinctions between our "norm" and yours. And though we Aspies are told that we are the black and white thinkers, I would argue that sometimes it is the neurotypical world (especially parents and teachers) that labels one viewpoint "normal" and the other "abnormal." I'll agree with "atypical," smile at "sometimes quirky," and cheer for "occasionally breathtakingly brilliant." But "wrong" is just, well, "wrong." Life – its comforts, joys, and challenges – is all profoundly relative.

Fabulous wall art, greeting cards, even coffee mugs entreat us all to "be bold...be random...be yourself." Hey, I am all for that. Paraphrasing a poster from my classroom, "well-behaved [people] rarely make history." But in reality, blending in is a whole lot easier. It takes guts to play the game if everyone else is playing poker and you show up with Monopoly pieces. Let's be honest, folks – Asperger's isn't for sissies. That's why perspective is so important...it's the permission we give ourselves as parents and teachers to whine, to pat our own backs, to occasionally cringe at our own kids' behavior, and to cry at the heroism of the smallest moments no one else even notices. As Boston artist Leigh Standley (www.curlygirldesign.com) scrawled into one of her illustrations, "I am fairly certain that given a cape and a nice tiara, I could save the world." Amen, sister.

No one signs up to give birth to a child with special needs, be they physical, psychological or both. I know – we have the gamut at our house. For whatever reason, that has not been hard for me to accept. My thought has been that "Why me?" could always be turned around into "Why not me?" But what to do if a parent or teacher doesn't want to make the life changes that an Asperkid requires? Not everyone enjoys structure; not everyone wants a schedule. I'm not mincing words or sugar-coating – life is not what you expect it will be. It's no surprise to me that so many marriages buckle under the financial, emotional, and logistical pressures. Who expects a trampoline in the living room? I can promise it wasn't part of my original decor. Even my perspective on my own priorities – whom did my house need to serve, imaginary judgmental guests or the kids who live here – had to change. In the end, the short bouncy people won.

As the parent or caretaker of an Asperkid, you will bump up against limits of comfort zones you never knew you had – and maybe some you won't want to admit you discovered. How many times can you hear your Asperkid make the same odd vocalization without going cuckoo? I'm an Aspie myself, and I can promise I am just as bonkers as you are after having all three of my Asperkids monologuing at me as you would be. It's OK. You're allowed. But you do have to watch how you show it.

As a young child, I would often go with my mother to the town pool during the summertime. She was a stay-at-home mom, and wanted some "grown-up time" chatting with the other moms on beach blankets. That is perfectly rational, healthy, and (as a mommy now, myself) understandable. But times were different back around 1980; nobody had ever heard of Asperger's, let alone coached parents on how to handle their kids. So my mom had a problem. She had a child in tow who didn't really want to be at the busy, hot pool. Still, she loves the water and couldn't imagine why I was so miserable there – so off we went, most every day. Very clearly, I can recall that almost as soon as we spread out our towels, my mom would shoo me away with her hand, telling me to "Just go play!" And my heart would sink.

The towels were surrounded by itchy grass or hot pavement. The bathrooms were echoing and slick. I didn't have friends there, and I couldn't just join in with some group of strangers. What the heck was I supposed to do, exactly? I was self-conscious and clueless as to where she wanted me to go, and had a million examples already in my mind of messing up socially – why put myself in harm's way again? The worst part was, though, that I took her dismissal as rejection. In my mind, even my mom didn't want me. Without a plan, I'd either head to the playground alone or sit beside her and read – which she said "looked weird." And though she couldn't know, those words hurt more than anything else. Feeling that we have let down our parents is a pain anyone can understand. But feeling that one's innate self is a let-down just slays you.

To be truthful, a lifetime of comments between then and now in which people I loved harshly criticized my social skills (with good intentions) has often brought that sense of rejection to bear. In her own way, my mom was trying to tell me that I was messing up. She made up stories with my Cabbage Patch Kids in which the redhead was a bossy smarty-pants whom no one really liked; the blonde doll was cute, likeable, and funny – everyone's favorite. Did I mention my mom was blonde? I know that her intent was to try to show why one personality was better received than the other. And I know that she really never gave thought to my misery at the pool – she just wanted some (well-deserved) time with adults. At the time, though, I couldn't see her perspective, and she didn't explain it to me. Everyone was expecting everyone else to read minds, and no one succeeded.

One day after school during the year I was in ninth grade, my social studies teacher spied me walking outside with some other students. He hollered across the campus lawn, "Oh, Miss Cook! I didn't realize you had friends!" Really? Was that supposed to help? Though things had turned around socially in just a year or two, when my friends were out of town on a class trip, I wouldn't chance a trip to the lunch room. The words of all those years took their toll, so I chose to eat my lunch alone, at the edge of the woods outside the high school. Odds are that I would've been welcome at another table quite readily. But in my mind, I was still that kid being called out by a teacher or spurned at the pool. So, I hid. And later, I got hit.

By the time I'd grown into the alluring redhead, pretty and popular years later, I also had it in my head that I was difficult to love, that I should be grateful for whoever took me on. I was living out a stereotype – a script – to prove to myself and to anyone else that I wasn't a social failure anymore. Never letting my perfect grade point average drop, I labeled myself in sorority letters and a cheerleading uniform – costumes of acceptance. I was serenaded by a bevvy of fraternity boys as their president, my boyfriend, brought flowers and jewelry up a ladder to my bedroom window – quite the public romantic pronouncement. I was selected by my peers as a student leader. Yet there was a dark side to that perfect picture. My varsity athlete, crazy-smart, guitar-playing boyfriend was also abusive. To me, it seemed a fair trade, even deserved. A bruise or intimate degradation in exchange for tolerating me – difficult to love, over-sensitive, and weird as I'd learned I must be. Such is the experience of an inordinate number of Aspergirls. I am not predicting the same danger for your children. Just know that "sticks and stones will break my bones, but names will never hurt me" is a total bunch of hogwash.

In my younger years, I held a lot of resentment toward my dad for walking away when I cried and toward my mom for so clearly misunderstanding me. But time has taught perspective. I know now that while they couldn't understand the limits of my comfort zones, neither could I understand theirs. My mom wanted things to be easy for me in the ways that they had been for her. She had no idea how to make that happen. In the meanwhile, she also wanted a happy life for herself. That's only fair. And sometimes, being courageous means doing the best you can. I know there were times I embarrassed her. I didn't mean to, but I'm sure I did. Yet oddly enough, when I wrote this book, my mom quoted a line from the movie, *The Help* (2011). "Sometimes courage skips a generation," she repeated. "You, I think, are courageous." I will remember that until the day I die.

As I listen at parent groups or to teachers, I hear such a "spectrum" of emotions: regret, weariness, determination. What if you don't want a home that runs on a schedule or if favorite passtimes make your Asperkid miserable? What if a colleague feels that adapting a classroom to support an Asperkid is simply coddling her? The only answer I can give you from "the inside" is that in very real ways, our futures are in your hands. Your words, gestures, and attitudes – we pick up much more of them than you know. And we know when we've let you down. So please be careful with your Asperkids.

Teaching us to be organized or how to play may be isolating, inconvenient, and tedious; our "mommy and daddy" friends don't have to do the same. They are rushing off to sports games, not therapy sessions. You will probably feel jealous of their parenting experiences, shortchanged by the sacrifices being asked of you, and even resentful of the attention Asperkids demand. Acknowledge any shame, grief or bitterness privately (ideally with professional guidance), and deal with them. Yes, you get to be angry things didn't work out as you'd planned, or that you aren't sufficiently appreciated or feel left out. You get to be tired and frustrated. You deserve friends, especially other spectrum parents who will *know* what you mean when you say meltdown or long day. You need days off, people to pitch in and let you be you whenever and however possible. It takes courage to accept the circumstances life hands us – it takes even greater courage to re-examine our expectations, and reframe our imagined lives. The house may have to be laid out differently to accommodate sensory needs (again, I refer to the trampoline in my living room!). Budgeting will surely have to change. Dreams of being part of a "regular" school community – as important to parents as to kids – may not turn out quite as planned.

It is OK to feel disappointed, overwhelmed, and confused by everyone telling you what to do (or what not to do). The "edge" of the comfort zone, my foot! Who expects to pick out an occupational therapist when other parents are choosing a preschool (which we *also* have to do)? Sometimes, the most difficult act of all is to stop and say, "Help. I can't do this alone." That doesn't mean you fail. I promise. Take it from perfectionist OCD mommy here. Ironically, at other times, the brave decision is to actually pull back.

We parents are bombarded by therapists of every kind – well-educated, well-intentioned people who sincerely want to help our kids be the best they can be. And, of course, each and every specialist feels that her arena is the most important. But occupational therapy (OT), speech therapy, play therapy, psychology, applied behavior analysis (ABA), dialectical behavior therapy (DBT), oxygen chambers, nutritional changes, social skills groups, animal therapy, music therapy, vision therapy, listening therapy, and a cadre of academic tutors cannot *all* feasibly be most important. One of the most common questions I'm asked by other parents is which service is the most important, and which can be dropped from the overstressed kid, schedule, pocketbook, and family life? The honest answer is that there is no answer. I have found that at various times, OT took precedence for one child while talk therapy (with a psychologist) was most important for another. Like a triage team on perpetual duty, we Asper-parents face a lifetime of perpetual choices between which needs are the most pronounced at present, and which can be put off for a while.

Women know that from the moment a pregnancy is announced, everyone has an opinion about something – including strangers on the street. The same is true in the world of autism/Asperger's. What is miraculously potent for one child may be completely ineffective for another, and conversations about said intervention will go on ad nauseam. The point is that there *is* no right answer. There is each parent's right answer, right now. It takes great courage to honor that place of trusting your gut, and this really must be respected as one of the few ways we Asper-parents have any sense of control. And please don't hide those big, fat feelings from your Asperkids, lest they blame themselves. Admit that even moms, dads, and teachers don't have all the answers. What we must have, though, is love and acceptance big enough for both of us, adult and child.

Once someone becomes a parent, her life is no longer her own entirely. But for most folks, there are breaks – getaways with friends, date nights with a spouse, maybe just dinner at a neighborhood pub. Once someone becomes the parent of an Aspie, for better or worse, life is absolutely and centrally about that child. It takes a while to grieve altered life plans, and reframe personal definitions of success, recreation and communication. Adults will have to learn to speak without idioms – or at least be prepared to explain them. Visual schedules will be everywhere. Anticipate meltdowns over kids getting in or out of the car in the "incorrect" sequence. Teachers will have to learn to understand why a student may absolutely *need* to spin or chew gum, even if it's "against the rules." Parents will have to learn to relearn ingrained concepts of discipline, and endure advice from everyone in the family. It's only fair to tell you to prepare for all of the above. It's scary. But it is reality. And it's essential that those who will play a role in the lives of Asperkids are ready.

An Asperkid needs proud champions who will insist, without being asked and without hesitation, that she is precious just exactly as she is. She is just a child, still developing a sense of self-worth. The life skills you teach now go far beyond playing or collaborating, organizing or arranging, compromising or coaching; when combined with your supportive attitude, those lessons directly impact an Asperkid's self-concept, and determine what kind of treatment she will accept from employers, spouses, and friends for the rest of her life. "Being brave," we explained to our daughter in some doctor's office along the line, "means feeling afraid, but doing it anyway." And that's a truth you have to teach by example.

For Aspies, almost everything in life is outside of our comfort zone. It's no wonder titles like *Raising Martians* (Muggleton 2011) and *Wrong Planet* (www.wrongplanet.net) abound. Nothing here quite fits us. That's why kids break down as they do or have such awful panic attacks. Rules aren't consistent, people don't say what they mean, and sensory overload is a matter of daily existence. Being perfectionists who often see the world in blacks and whites, playing to the one critic in the audience rather than the theater full of cheers, we have to call upon courage constantly, and in times the rest of the world takes utterly for granted. Once neurotypical folks appreciate our perspective – grasping the effort of standing at the edge of belonging, and never quite knowing if we are "passing" – it becomes easier to respond to behaviors compassionately, albeit firmly. The world still expects manners, deadlines, and accuracy. And we are capable of all three.

In fact, I have seen that in life's most acute moments, we Aspies have an advantage. We've gotten used to life outside our comfort zones. So, when situations call for courage, we can be pretty good at "putting on our big girl panties and dealing with it." In dark hospital nights, speaking with parents of other chronically ill children, other parents have wondered at my positive tenacity. As my husband says, "It is what it is. You do what you have to do." I agree, and I'm fairly certain that attitude comes from a life of just hanging in there.

The simple truth is that Aspies get more practice being brave than almost anyone because the whole neurotypical world is outside of our comfort zone. My husband is a police officer. And while the bravest moment of his life took place at work, it wasn't on the streets. It was in the employee parking lot. He'd spent the day "volunteered" by his sergeant for a class on domestic violence calls, and apparently, he'd taken quite a shine to the redheaded instructor in the short black skirt-suit. Now class was over. And though anyone would call him handsome, and though his air is authoritative and firm, he found himself sitting outside in his own car, staring at the sunglasses in his hands, having a full-blown panic attack. Though he didn't know it at the time, social anxiety was paralyzing him from just talking to that girl. To me. He could strap on a bulletproof vest or storm a drug den. But he will tell you that it was only divine intervention that gave him the strength to get up and march back in, pretending to have forgotten his sunglasses in the classroom. And of course, I was awfully glad to see him come back.

A poignant truth about Aspies is that we have an uncanny knowledge of what we can do well, and what we can't. That can work in our favor. When asked if I am scared speaking before large audiences or writing this book, the honest answer is "no." I know I can talk to groups comfortably and connect with them. I know that I can rapidly write my truth as if I were speaking to a dear friend. Words are my friends.

I have also learned (all too acutely) what I am *not* good at. I also know that, despite a good heart and positive intentions, I never should have been the Parent-Teacher Committee chair at my kids' preschool. Reading personalities, blending perspectives/needs, interpersonal drama, and fuzzy social rules were not what I should have been trying to do. For my whole life, I have tried to be everything to everyone. That meant, necessarily, that I always failed at something, which devastated me. But the blessing of knowing I am an Aspergirl is that, at last, I am coming to drop the facade of social proficiency. There is a gray area. Lack of easy success does not equal personal failure; I get that now. But to an Asperkid, that is a discovery waiting a long way off.

Afraid of disappointing others, being embarrassed or left out, we avoid the things we inherently know aren't our strengths: social situations, even some academic or professional tasks. That's why people so often think Aspies are content to be on the sidelines.

While sometimes we do want to be by ourselves, often we don't get involved because we already know we'll fail, feel the sting of rejection, or the ache of exclusion. We'd simply rather not subject ourselves.

Think about it. There's an expression on greeting cards, "What would you do if you knew you couldn't fail?" That's wonderful inspiration. But what about if you knew you would? Or at least were so paralyzed by the trauma of past hurts that you didn't have it in you to try one more time? For us, simply living every day in a world where we miss vast chunks of communication (body language) and endure sensory overload dictates that we *have* to constantly step outside of our comfort zones. Yes, everyone has to be brave to get a job, make a friend, fall in love. But that's occasionally, not incessantly. We Aspies have to arm ourselves with social scripts and self-talk mantras just to get through a Monday morning meeting.

My undergraduate major was in a topic called "American Civilization," a department that is, essentially, a hybrid of history, literature, popular culture, theatre, religion, music, material culture (furniture styles, etc.), and socioeconomics. The way I most often found myself describing the genre was that graduates would become so well versed in what it meant to "be American" in a certain era, that given a time machine, we could plunk ourselves down and blend in, comfortably knowing everything from what specific songs were the biggest hits of the day to what games kids played or what clothing styles were all the rage. Each student had to select a time period in which to specialize, to understand, to "fit into" seamlessly. Which did I choose? Late twentieth century America; please note that I graduated in 1997. In other words, without understanding why, I chose my own society to analyze the most deeply. Furthermore, I wrote an honors thesis on Barbie, a "post war didactic tool of modern feminism." Translation? Why was the Barbie doll such an unprecedented hit, what did that say about what American moms wanted to teach their daughters, and how did those messages show up as those little girls (like me!) grew up?

Point is this: I made a major out of figuring out my own culture. It might never be instinctive, but it could be intellectualized. Intuitively, I couldn't read my own society. But made into a formal anthropological study, issues as complicated as sexuality and body image became a well-ordered, conclusive academic thesis. And that neurotypical world, once better understood, is not nearly so scary.

Aspie minds are set up to follow rules. We adore purpose and intention. We seek order, rationale, resolution. Yet to survive in this neurotypical world, we have to do the complete opposite – we have to socialize, empathize, and intellectualize in ways that are thoroughly unnatural to us. It's no wonder that when we find a friend or significant other, we cling (sometimes too) tightly; he or she is a lifeline. It's no wonder that Aspies immerse themselves in special interests, or fall into routines and patterns. Known quantities act like waypoints, restful beacons after the chaos of hectic schedules, unpredictable social scenes, and fluid rules.

Parents and teachers of Aspie kids know that a breakdown is hard to watch, let alone endure (as are the stares if it's in public). On behalf of our kids, though, who often bear life histories of feeling left out or not good enough, I ask you to take a breath and try to reframe your perception of the outbursts. More often than not, the issue isn't pure opposition; it's obsessive thoughts that won't allow us to concentrate on more important matters, or internalization of some critique as a commentary on our worth. That Asperkid may have braved some hidden fear, and failed again. Or even if a day has seemed ideal, a wonderful playdate may have taken so much energy that there is no emotional bandwidth left to spare. What you are seeing in the tears and rage is: "I am tired. Tired of trying all the time, being brave all the time, working at everything, everywhere I go." Being punitive won't help. Being empathetic may. Giving room to decompress will, for sure.

For us, families and professionals who love Asperkids, simply advocating for a child may lead to personal or professional exclusion. It isn't comfortable. It takes courage to tell an authority figure that something isn't quite right, and argue your point. It takes courage to listen and learn about Asperger's, even if a friend, spouse or extended family member is dismissive. For the kids themselves, it's much more often about small, daily triumphs, rather than grandiose gestures. More often than not, these tasks are easy for you, though they aren't for us. Climbing through a playground tunnel may be terrifying. Heck, just going to the playground may be terrifying. Last summer, I discovered a book of poetry I'd written when I was 12. The last two lines read:

> Please! Don't roll your eyes at what I say
> You were my friend just yesterday.

During the devestation of World War II, Winston Churchill famously said, "Never, never, never, never give up." I think Aspies don't really have a choice, if we want to thrive. Many times, people ask for strength, forgetting that this means they will have to choose to be strong in the face of trial. Or they may pray for joy, not realizing that they may have to choose to see the silver lining inside of a very dark cloud. One's entire life's journey may be fashioned not on the circumstances we are dealt but the way in which we choose to frame them. On behalf of little Asperkids everywhere, I ask you to sing the praises of a moment of flexible thinking. Or a chance taken in admitting your own confusion. Proust famously said that the "real voyage of discovery consists...in seeing with new eyes." If that's so, thank you, teachers, parents, and caregivers, for recognizing the power of perspective in a nearsighted world. With a good set of glasses, *all* of us – Aspies, parents, and teachers – can see one another a whole lot more clearly.

8 CONCLUSION
My Father's Legacy

Four years ago, my father died at the age of 62 from lung cancer. He was born and passed without ever having heard of Asperger's. And, while no psychologist can travel back in time to conduct testing or make a diagnosis, it's very obvious to me where my Asperger's comes from.

My dad was the youngest of three children, a successful attorney, and married to my mom for 36 years; he loved baseball, bad sci fi, fishing, and spy novels. For as long as I could recall, his dream was to buy a boat, something he achieved at a relatively young age. At the marina, I saw my dad come alive for the first time. Within a world of charts and navigation, Jimmy Buffett music and GPS technology, a whole social circle existed, full of folks who shared a passion for his special interest. Often, if I came home to visit from college for a weekend, he would spend the whole time on the boat, instead. Back then, I was insulted. But in hindsight, I understand. He had found his nirvana, and would always go to the place where he was most comfortable being Joe.

He was painfully shy, often rocked back and forth clumsily during conversations, and relied on scotch or cigarettes to get him through social engagements. When he saw me struggle, asking Santa for a friend, or crying about another social blunder, it was just too much. He would turn and walk out of the room. Time passed, and I rather adeptly learned to mimic scripts, faking social ease with finesse. I charmed my father, too, and he was elated. "I'm so glad,"

I remember him saying, a glass in one hand and tears in his eyes, "that you don't have the trouble with people that I do." What a pure expression of love. We all want better for our children, and my dad didn't want me to hurt as he had on so many occasions. I remember being somewhat pleased and yet also sad that I'd so easily fooled him; but the relief in his eyes burned an impression on my heart that remains today. Let him think I haven't been where he has. That I won't yet hurt as he has. Give him that.

On one particularly trying night a few years later, my dad told me something that I will never forget. "Jenny," he whispered, "I think you understand me better than anyone." This was no dig on my mom, his sisters, or his boating friends. Looking back, I think he'd finally realized that we were more alike than he'd hoped. But he didn't sound sorry for it, at least not in that moment. On that blustery evening, my dad felt connected.

The greatest gift of my own Asperger's diagnosis, made only a year ago, is that the previous 34 years of my life finally make sense. My mother often told me that she hoped someday I would be happy; and while it may sound strange, I told her that I didn't want to be. Happy, it seemed, was transient, a passing mood like being sad or worried. I didn't want temporary. Contentedness sounded a whole lot better. Though I had no real idea how to get there, being "content" implied a deep, unwavering satisfaction and pleased acceptance. And that, I thought, sounded awfully good. It turned out that "how to get there" was discovering that I am an Aspie. And, with self-awareness, reflection, and purpose, I can now say I was right – contentedness is awfully good.

Understanding has changed everything. I would never criticize a blind person for coloring outside of the lines. He can't see. It's not a reflection of his effort or value as a person. He just can't do what's being asked. Nor would I ask my DVD to act as a GPS. It's hardwired to show movies, not to give navigational tips. I can yell at the dang thing or smack it or call the maker, but that DVD player is not going to suddenly give me driving directions. It's not supposed to. In exactly the same way, I understand that I am psychologically blind in many ways. When, socially, I have "colored outside the lines," it's OK. I couldn't see the lines to start off with. Like the DVD machine,

I'm fully functional – but, at least socially, I'm not hardwired to do what is asked of me.

Diagnosis has allowed me to give myself the gift of forgiveness for being precocious when I meant to be endearing, clingy when I meant to be loyal, or naive when, well, I was naive. I am not now, nor have I ever been, able to "play games"; I don't lie, can't be duplicitous, and I literally don't know how to be conniving or manipulative. My mind doesn't allow me to even see how to do those things. I'm no angel – I'm an Aspie. What you see is what you get. I say what I mean, and I mean what I say – no more, no less. That's too simple, too real for much of the world, but it is me.

Realizing that I am an Aspergirl has also freed me to ask for help in ways I wouldn't have otherwise. I've never been too proud to look for assistance, but oftentimes, I wouldn't realize that I needed it until I'd already goofed. Now I know to approach a friend for help on interpersonal issues; understanding my Asperger's, they don't think it's odd to be asked. In that sense, diagnosis has also allowed my friends to make sense of the times I've seemed distant, curt, or uninterested, and to know that it is not my love for them that wavers – only my focus.

The present is better than the past, and the future will be better than the present. So many of the choices in the ways my husband and I parent our kids come from our own experiences growing up Aspie. We know what it is to feel deficient, other, less. Yet we look at our Asperkids in wonder and awe: there is so much that is beautiful about them. They are brilliant books, waiting to be opened, full of undiscovered perspectives, truths, and feelings. And they are so fragile. Like wolves, children and adults alike can sense the weak among the group, and they will attack.

I suppose that I am like the tacky peanut butter filling in an Aspie sandwich, stuck between my dad's generation, and my kids'. My father never got the chance to understand his own set of challenges and aptitudes in the light of "you are exactly as you were meant to be" rather than in comparison to what he thought he should be. For the first 34 years of my life, neither did I. But now, everything is different – for me and for my children. We know who we are: we are people with passions, fears, grief, and hope that is as real and potent and valuable as yours, even if it looks or sounds or acts a little bit different. We are as we should be.

I deeply hope that as you've read this book, parents have recognized your children, teachers have recognized your students, and maybe some of you have even recognized yourselves. Every hurtful moment I've lived, every humiliation I've endured, will have been worth it if I have made anything better for the millions of Asperkids out there. Just as my own life informs the purposeful choices I make in educating and supporting my Asperkids, may it be so for yours.

The tools are yours now. You have walked alongside me and taken a front-row seat to my life as an Aspie. You have learned the why's behind the strategies, and have the resources to make them work for your own Asperkid. Speak the language of the special interest. Appeal to a preference for concrete learning. Find detours when obstacles stand between your Asperkid and the rest of the world. And be sure to give your child the very real skills he needs to feel competent and confident whether he is teaching quantum mechanics or helping his family clean up after dinner.

I am Jane and Joe's daughter. I am John's wife. I am Maura, Sean, and Gavin's mom. Their names haven't been mentioned a lot in the book because, while details may change from one family to the next, there are common themes that bind all of our stories. My dad never got to understand why he was as he was. But I did, and his grandchildren will. So, somewhere on cerulean blue waters, Joe is undoubtedly at the helm of a boat. I hope he can see me, his "Little Red." He was right, I am a lot like him. And my kids are a lot like me. And we are all as we should be – perfectly content being, and speaking, Aspie.

REFERENCES

Books and papers

Attwood, T. (2010) "Personal observations." Autism/Asperger's Super-Conference, Charlotte, NC, October 21–22, 2010.

Britton, L. (1992) *Montessori Play and Learn: A Parent's Guide to Purposeful Play from Two to Six*. New York: Three Rivers Press.

Baker, J. (2010) "Personal observations." Autism/Asperger's Super-Conference, Charlotte, NC, October 21–22, 2010.

Carley, M.J. (2008) *Asperger's from the Inside Out: A Supportive and Practical Guide for Anyone with Asperger's Syndrome*. New York: Perigree.

Clark, J. (2010) *Asperger's in Pink: A Mother and Daughter Guidebook for Raising (or Being) a Girl with Asperger's*. Arlington, TX: Future Horizons.

Dawkins, R. (1976) *The Selfish Gene*. Oxford: Oxford University Press.

Dickinson, E. (1998) "I dwell in possibility" (#657). *The Poems of Emily Dickinson*, Ralph W. Franklin, ed. Cambridge, MA: Belknap Press of Harvard University Press.

Duffy, M. (2008) *Math Works: Montessori Math and the Developing Brain*. Hollidaysburg, PA: Parent Child Press.

Gardner, H. (1993) *Frames of Mind: The Theory of Multiple Intelligences*. New York: Basic Books.

Gladwell, M. (2002) *The Tipping Point: How Little Things Can Make a Big Difference*. Boston, MA: Back Bay Books.

Grandin, T. (2006) *Thinking in Pictures: And Other Reports from My Life with Autism*, 2nd edn. New York: Vintage.

Hemingway, E. (1952) *The Old Man and the Sea*. New York: Charles Scribner's Sons.

Holub, J. and Williams, S. (2010) *Athena the Brain: Goddess Girls, Book #1*. New York: Aladdin.

Jackson, L. (2002) *Freaks, Geeks, and Asperger's Syndrome: A User Guide to Adolescence*. London: Jessica Kingsley Publishers.

Lewis, C.S. (1955) *The Magician's Nephew: The Chronicles of Narnia*. London: J. Lane.

McClure, W. (2011) *The Wilder Life: My Adventures in the Lost World of Little House on the Prairie*. New York: Riverhead.

Montessori, M. (1949) *The Absorbent Mind*. New York: Holt, Reinhart & Winston.

Muggleton, J. (2011) *Raising Martians – from Crash-landing to Leaving Home: How to Help a Child with Asperger Syndrome or High-functioning Autism*. London: Jessica Kingsley Publishers.

Pitamic, M. (2004) *Teach Me to Do It Myself: Montessori Activities for You and Your Child*. Hauppauge, NY: Barron's.

Riordan, R. (2006) *The Lightning Thief (Percy Jackson and the Olympians, Book 1)*. New York: Hyperion.

Shakespeare, W. (1600) *Romeo and Juliet*. London.

Simone, R. (2010) *Aspergirls: Empowering Females with Asperger Syndrome*. London: Jessica Kingsley Publishers.

Stewart, M. (2006) *Martha Stewart's Homekeeping Handbook: The Essential Guide to Caring for Everything in Your Home*. New York: Clarkson Potter.

Wilder, L.I. (1932) *The Little House in the Big Woods*. New York: HarperCollins.

Songs and movies

"For Good" (2003) Song from *Wicked: The Untold Story of the Witches of Oz*. Musical with music and lyrics by Stephen Schwartz.

Ingenious Minds: Temple Grandin (2010) Video written and directed by Toy Newkirk. Screaming Flea Productions.

The Birdcage (1996) Motion picture directed by Mike Nichols. MGM/United Artists.

"The Downeaster 'Alexa'" (1990) Song by Billy Joel. Columbia Records.

The Help (2011) Motion picture directed by Tate Taylor. Touchstone Pictures.

The Indian in the Cupboard (1995) Motion picture directed by Frank Oz. Columbia Pictures.

The Princess and the Frog (2009) Motion picture directed by Ron Clements and John Musker. Walt Disney Animation Studios.

The Wizard of Oz (1939) Motion picture directed by Victor Fleming. MGM Studios.

"Whatever Lola Wants" (1955) Song from Damn Yankees. Musical with music and lyrics by Richard Adler and Jerry Ross.

"Where Do You Start Your Letters?" (2008) Song by Jan Olsen. www.hwtears.com/files/click/HWT-ROCK-lyrics-Where-Do-You-Start-Your-Letters.pdf

Websites

All websites were accessed December 1, 2011.

Curly Girl Design (Leigh Standley)
www.curlygirldesign.com

FlyLady.net (Marla Cilley)
www.flylady.net

Handwriting Without Tears (Jan Olsen)
www.hwtears.com

ShillerMath: How Kids Learn Math ("ShillerMath CD #1: Exchange," Larry Shiller)
www.shillermath.com

TouchMath (Multisensory Teaching, Learning Math Tools)
www.touchmath.com

RESOURCES

Learning and play supplies

Absorbent Minds Montessori
A UK-based provider of Montessori equipment to schools, homeschoolers, and parents; website features an "Ideas Bank" of practical life activities.
www.absorbentminds.co.uk

Alison's Montessori
Educational, creative supplies, and materials.
www.alisonsmontessori.com

Crafts 4 Kids
A "rightly fussy" specialist online toy store featuring only products "of great design and quality, offering genuine skill transference as well as…being brilliant fun."
www.crafts4kids.co.uk

FlipFold
The FlipFold laundry folding board is a brightly colored folding tool for clothing, bedding, and towels. It comes in multiple sizes, is easy to use, and features rubber bumpers and cushions for easy handling. A sure bet to help kids feel successful at an otherwise tricky life skill.
www.flipfold.com

For Small Hands
"Real child-size tools, books, and educational materials; designed for family use in the Montessori tradition."
www.forsmallhands.com

Handwriting Without Tears (Jan Olsen)
"A complete handwriting curriculum for all children."
www.hwtears.com

Kid Advance
Supplier of Montessori materials and other learning products.
www.kidadvance.com

Lego® Education
Hands-on Lego® activities and projects for science, information and control technology, design and technology, English, math, and humanities.
www.legoeducation.com
http://educationuk.lego.com

Lindamood-Bell Learning Centers (UK, US, and Australia)
Providing one-to-one sensory-cognitive support of the skills underlying successful reading, spelling, and comprehension.
www.lindamoodbell.com

Montessori AMI Primary Guide
Links to free materials and videos on how to use Montessori materials.
www.infomontessori.com

Montessori for Everyone
High-quality, printable PDFs for home, homeschools, and schools.
www.montessoriforeveryone.com

Montessori Research and Development
Curriculum materials and teacher guides.
www.montessorird.com

Montessori Services
"A resource for preparing the child's environment."
www.montessoriservices.com

Museum Tour
"Educational toy, book, and learning game catalog founded by former President of the Oregon Museum of Science and Industry."
www.museumtour.com

Orton-Gillingham Institute for Multi-Sensory Education
Offers a multi-sensory approach that provides students the
opportunity for success, and benefits every learner.
www.orton-gillingham.com

ShillerMath Math Songs
By Ron Brown, Nancy Brown, and Larry Shiller.
www.shillermath.com

TouchMath
"Multisensory teaching, learning math tools make math fun!"
www.touchmath.com

Young Explorers
Creative educational projects, kits, and toys.
www.youngexplorers.com

Great books for parents, teachers, and kids

American Girl Library social books: Middleton, WI: American Girl.
> Criswell, P.K. (2006) *Friends: Making Them and Keeping Them.*
> Criswell, P.K. (2008) *A Smart Girl's Guide to Friendship Troubles.*
> Criswell, P.K. (2008) *Stand Up for Yourself and Your Friends.*
> Criswell, P.K. (2011) *A Smart Girl's Guide to Knowing What to Say.*
> Madison, L. (2010) *The Care and Keeping of You Collection.*
> Phillips, B.W. (2009) *Oh Brother!...Oh Sister!: A Sister's Guide to Getting Along.*
> Timmons, B. (2005) *Yikes! A Smart Girl's Guide to Surviving Tricky, Sticky, Icky Situations.*

Attwood, T. (2007) *The Complete Guide to Asperger's Syndrome.*
London: Jessica Kingsley Publishers.

Baker, J. (2001) *The Social Skills Picture Book: Teaching
Communication, Play and Emotion.* Arlington, TX: Future Horizons.

Britton, L. (1992) *Montessori Play and Learn: A Parent's Guide to
Purposeful Play from Two to Six.* New York: Three Rivers Press.

Duffy, M. (2008) *Math Works: Montessori Math and the Developing Brain*. Hollidaysburg, PA: Parent Child Press.

Pitamic, M. (2004) *Teach Me to Do It Myself: Montessori Activities for You and Your Child*. Hauppauge, NY: Barron's.

Simone, R. (2010) *Aspergirls: Empowering Females with Asperger Syndrome*. London: Jessica Kingsley Publishers.

Technology and online

Cozi
Online and mobile family organizer that coordinates and color-codes individuals' calendars, to-do's, and shopping lists in real-time (and it's free!).
www.cozi.com

Dance Mat Typing
Simply the best keyboarding tutorial anywhere.
www.bbc.co.uk/schools/typing

FlyLady.net
"Your personal online coach to help you gain control of your house and home."
www.flylady.net

Montessorium
"A new type of classroom, a continuum of proven and tested Montessori principles and materials, in the hands of children." Montessori tools redesigned for iPad, iPhone, iTouch.
www.montessorium.com

NOOK and Kindle e-reader technology
www.barnesandnoble.com and *www.amazon.com* or *www.amazon.co.uk*

And there simply is nothing better than the iPad for its intuitive genius.